THE MENTORING ORGANIZATION

Gordon F. Shea

CRISP Learning

Menlo Park, California

Portions of this book appeared in an earlier form in a booklet in the series, *American Management Association Briefings—Mentoring: Helping Employees Reach Their Full Potential* by Gordon F. Shea.

Managing Editor: George Young
Editor: Sal Glynn
Cover Design and Production: Fifth Street Design
Book Design and Production: Nicole Phillips
Printer:

ISBN 1-56052-673-4
03 04 05 06 10 9 8 7 6 5 4 3 2 1

Library of Congress Cataloging-in-Publication Data

Shea, Gordon F., 1925-
  The mentoring organization / Gordon F. Shea.
    p. cm.
  ISBN 1-56052-673-4 (pbk.)
  1. Mentoring in business. I. Title.
  HF5385.S553 2003
  658.3'124--dc22

                        2003015668

TABLE OF CONTENTS

INTRODUCTION

The word "mentor" comes from Homer's epic work, *The Odyssey*. When Odysseus, King of Ithaca, went to fight in the Trojan War, he entrusted his friend, Mentor, with the education of his son, Telemachus. Mentor's task was to educate, train, and develop the youngster to fulfill his birthright and become king of Ithaca.

Mentoring was already practiced worldwide eons before the Greek poet Homer gave this special art of people development its name some 3500 years ago. Archeologists, anthropologists, and sociologists suggest there is evidence of mentoring occurring among flint knappers, cave artists, and religious leaders as early as the Stone Age.

As the ages passed, mentoring evolved to meet new societal, family, and organizational needs. This developmental process is still going on today, but at an ever-faster pace, particularly in business, academia, community, and government. Mentoring is becoming more democratic and is especially being used to help develop a wide variety of employees of varied skill levels, backgrounds, and job responsibilities.

People are looking beyond just a training program and realizing that employees mentoring employees can have long-lasting effects on each mentee, paying dividends to the sponsoring organization for decades to come. Much of what passes between mentor and mentee is informal knowledge, supplementing and complementing more formal learning and serving a variety of unique needs in each relationship.

Many of the current mentoring programs are based on Industrial Age models, and are possibly counter-productive in the context of our emerging Information Age needs. It is critical that people develop the most advanced form of mentoring possible and build into their organizations the ability to update and improve programs as the art of mentoring evolves.

Since the mid-1980s, mentoring as an employee-development strategy has changed dramatically. This new form of helping people learn and perform better offers a wealth of management opportunities for organizational rejuvenation, competitive adaptation, and employee development.

Much of the change has occurred in response to significant developments in operational and technological advancements, evolution in local and world markets, and entirely new sets of workplace realities—from dealing with downsizing and delayering, to creating self-managed teams and purposefully changing corporate cultures. But many organizations appear to have missed a curve in the road. They are unaware of the newer models of mentoring and the promise they hold.

In 1984, we were just beginning to feel the impact of personal computers on nearly every desk, and just a decade later the Internet, e-mail, and the information age was in full swing. The impact of these and other developments on mentoring was profound. The main thrust was a significant growth in the use of mentoring and the emergence of some advanced models and more sophisticated practices.

A Different Way

A major electronics manufacturer created an Information Age mentoring program at their corporate headquarters. New corporate executives and personnel transferred from other divisions had to adapt quickly to a new fast-paced, top-level corporate culture. A diverse task force spearheaded by the human resources manager created an advanced two-pronged mentoring program. The formal program matched headquarter-based mentors with newcomers to bring their mentees to full participation and assimilation as quickly as possible. An informal mentor/mentee program on an ongoing basis was introduced so that every employee could participate in sophisticated mentoring relationships as their needs and inclinations dictated.

The formal program aimed at achieving immediate specific organizational results, as well as establishing the relationship foundations for more comprehensive and long-term mentee developmental benefits. In both programs, the relationship was based on a mutually developed agreement and terminated when the mentee's learning or performance objectives were met, unless a new or modified agreement was formulated.

A Decade of Development in the New Mentoring

To appreciate how mentoring changed and to understand how organizations have responded to that change, consider the results of two research studies, one conducted in 1984 and the other in early 1994. The first (1984) study polled human resources directors at 62 firms and 37 government agencies (federal, state, and local) in the greater Washington, DC/Baltimore area about their use of mentoring as an employee-development tool. The researcher drew his sample from a variety of private sector organizations (company sizes ranged from approximately 100 employees to more than 2,000), and he selected public sector agencies so that the response group would represent significant segments of government. For example, at the federal level, respondents came from agencies within the U.S. Department of Transportation and U.S. Department of Agriculture. At the state and local levels, it was the highway and police departments. (The researcher chose to use these organizational units because they were small enough so that someone near the top could answer specific questions.)

The researcher found in the 1984 study that the human resources directors had little specific knowledge about mentoring activities within their organizations. Many made vague references to their efforts in "encouraging informal mentoring." Six respondents (about 10 percent) said their firms did have mentoring programs in place. These respondents worked in large, stable, "old line" organizations that used mentoring in the following ways.

To initiate and orient new professional hires. The organizations matched these employees, usually referred to as interns, with higher level people outside of their "chain of command" for a period of three months to a year.

To develop high-potential personnel. The organizations singled out certain individuals to be "fast tracked" for management positions and often assigned them a mentor to help in their climb up the career ladder.

To assist in succession planning. Three organizations had an informal custom where management and executive personnel trained their successors. The mentors in these relationships were not actually trained to mentor; instead, they generally engaged in a "Copy what I do and how I do it" type of activity.

In contrast, the government sampling failed to reveal any meaningful patterns, with one exception: Many police departments promoted the mentoring of new personnel (especially personnel who were new to patrol) by experienced officers. Respondents from many of the other agencies seemed uncertain as to whether the organization did or did not use mentoring.

The 1994 study attempted to access the same organizations (six of the companies had disappeared, moved, or been absorbed by others, and two government units had merged with another organization). It produced substantial contrasts—of the 56 private firms that responded for a second time, one-third reported they had formal mentoring programs in place, and another third were actively exploring such programs. Of the 35 governmental agencies that responded for a second time, 17 said they had some form of mentoring in place, and 15 said they were exploring the possibilities.

Although the survey worked with a limited sample, the results mirror the nationwide growth in mentoring during this time. Even more interesting—and also a bit disturbing—is that in organizations that adopted some form of mentoring, half of the programs clearly resembled the Industrial Age model. Moreover, almost all the other organizations seemed to be struggling to adapt the old model to new needs. Very few demonstrated awareness that a more forward-looking model was available. The two approaches stand in sharp contrast. The contrasting models are shown in the two boxes that follow.

Characteristics of the Industrial Age Model

The Industrial Age model of mentoring is characterized by a single-minded focus on career advancement. The model assumes that all "eligible" employees are seeking to climb an organizational ladder within the tall, hierarchical, multi-layered, organization of the past. Other characteristics include:

The perception that a mentor is a protector and sponsor. This model reflects the medieval term "protégé" (literally, "the favored or protected one"). Historically, the protégé's career was placed in the hands of a more powerful advocate (who, ironically, sometimes used the protégé as a pawn in empire-building and office politics).

A tendency to clone look-alike, think-alike, and act-alike managers. This model encouraged managers to share a particular organizational vision and culture, and hold similar career aspirations.

A fundamentally elitist vision of mentoring. According to this model, mentoring was a strategy for assimilating "high potential" personnel, rather than using it as a tool for discovering or developing varied talents throughout the workforce.

The exclusion of broader, organizational concerns. Because of its emphasis on an individual's career-development goals, the Industrial Age model tended to overlook the importance of mentoring to organization development. This may explain why many upper-level managers resisted formal mentoring programs.

A preoccupation with the rationalization of work, logical problem solving, and the "dumbing down" of most jobs. During the Industrial Age, this preoccupation left little besides a paycheck for the millions of employees who either applied their imagination and talents to activities outside the workplace or simply never developed these facets of their abilities.

A tendency to characterize people by the work they do. Because of this myopic perception, companies that embraced the Industrial Age model often failed to explore the many facets of each employee's personality, aspirations, talents, and experience. (Today, companies that rely on the Industrial Age model often face the same problems.)

Companies were often left with a passive workforce and a rift between workers and management that was spanned only by the occasional use of informal (interpersonal) mentoring by a supervisor or technical or professional person who decided to help a (usually) younger or less-experienced subordinate.

Today's organizations need employee contribution and commitment—elements that are hardly brought out by such an outmoded and passive form of mentoring.

Characteristics of Information Age Mentoring

Information Age organizations use mentoring to improve the quality of employee work life, train in specialized technical skills, and adapt its operations in ways that take advantage of rapidly developing workforce diversity. These organizations hone each person's inner uniqueness and their special array of talents, experience and abilities. Typical goals are:

• Mentor training to enable a person to operate across the entire mentoring spectrum, meet short-term situational needs, and work within the context of both informal and formal mentoring relationships.

• Mentee training to help the learner build a "partnering" relationship with a mentor, take greater responsibility for self-development, and make more effective use of what a mentor can offer.

• A highly flexible and often voluntary system of mentoring where mentors and mentees decide if they can or should work together.

• A formal system that is non-burdensome, non-bureaucratic, and virtually self-managed. A mentoring coordinator identifies appropriate matches and leaves the task of forming the relationship up to the potential participants (often after each receives training in both roles).

• An intranet bulletin board system for mentees to list their needs and mentors list their skills and areas of special knowledge and experience. Participants find each other and form an effective match to meet their short-term or informal needs.
An internal communication system that allows mentor/mentee interactions as needs, opportunities, and questions arise.

• An open system that allows for multiple mentors or mentees arrangements, or for a given individual to serve as a mentor or mentee in informal relationships, or both, as the situation warrants.

• Many Human Resources departments loan training videos and provide workbooks to individuals and units that request them. The workbooks are used for self-study or by discussion groups to enhance mentor/mentee skills.

This sharing of information enables even small, remote units to engage in mentoring. As the system expands, it creates a greater sharing of employee ideas and knowledge. The process of *efficient information* flow focuses on the efficient sharing and transfer of skills and information on corporate best practices in a value-added context.

Informal training is characterized by its *democratic nature, egalitarianism,* and being *mentee-driven.* By offering informal mentor/mentee training in "lunch bag seminars," virtually every employee at a given location could in time engage in one or more effective mentoring relationships. Mentors and mentees are paired on meeting knowledge needs rather than on their relative rank and hierarchy. Switching from what the mentor can give, to what the mentee needs leads to an increased emphasis on mentee performance, more comprehensive mentor/mentee training, and a de-emphasis on "copy cat" learning.

Ten Potential Gains for the Organization

- The existence of a broad-based mentoring program strengthens the organization's image as being a caring, sharing, and helping community of employees.

- Mentoring offers a competitive edge in recruiting efforts, particularly in times and areas of labor shortages.

- Mentors can facilitate, strengthen, and often shorten the new employee's induction and orientation process.

- Mentoring supplements traditional and special employee training by helping such trainees quickly apply their learning and develop mastery of a subject.

- Research strongly indicates that a quality mentoring program significantly improves employee retention rates.

- A community of mentors in an organization creates a more open, cooperative, and receptive environment for fresh ideas, and for the quick and easy exchange of important information.

- A mentor's help often improves a new employee's per sonal productivity, internal motivation, and sense of responsibility for results.

- Mentoring can be used to build a more inclusive, equitable, and democratic work environment.

- Well-trained mentors learn to avoid many of the common negative and unproductive personal reasoning practices and behaviors such as "group think," rationalizing questionable proposals, or unfairly discounting the legitimate needs of other individuals or groups.

- A productive mentoring network in an organization improves the entity's quickness of response, adaptability to change, and the broad sharing of new and emerging opportunities.

Ten Possible Gains for the Mentor

- The mentor learns an important set of interpersonal, developmental, and leadership skills.

- Mentors expand and extend their personal network of learning-links within the organization so they can refer mentees to specialists when appropriate.

- Serving as a mentor enables professionals and other leaders to keep in touch with grassroots personnel.

- Mentors learn to recognize, encourage, and develop a wider variety of employee talents, abilities, and attributes.

- Mentoring adds a helping, mentee-focused dimension to the mentor's regular job activities.

- Mentoring provides an outlet for each person's innate altruism.

- Mentoring offers occasional variation, change, and even pleasant surprises to a mentor's regular working activities, and helps to keep them fresh.

- Being a mentor provides opportunities to invest directly in another person's success and reap the good feelings that come from their success.

- Mentoring enables a person to keep a current knowledge of changes in the workforce, the workplace, and the world from which their mentees come.

- A mentor learns from the engagement and exchange with the mentee, particularly from the mental exercise they perform when making new connections between their own experience and learning and that of the mentee.

Ten Possible Gains for the Mentee/Partner

- A mentee can use the existence of a developmental mentoring program as criteria for choosing among employers and/or employment options.

- A mentee can experience the sense of comfort and support that comes from having a knowledgeable and trained person to talk to about work issues.

- A mentee can access the special knowledge, view points, and experience that an insider has about the organization's history, objectives, practices, and culture.

- A mentee can create a personal and knowledgeable foundation for meeting present and future organizational work standards, social norms, and group contribution.

- A mentee can learn special mentee skills as well as gain knowledge and ideas about how to make the most of their mentoring experience.

- A mentee can gather, select, and remember lessons, quotable quotes, values, and beliefs from their mentor(s) that they consider suitable for themselves and applicable to other situations they may encounter.

- A mentee can become a more proactive person who seeks out and builds a personal network of "as needed" mentors who can round out their capabilities and help them to become more fully developed.

- A mentee can learn the lessons of self-managed career development and get help in constructing, detailing, developing, and carrying out their personal Individual Development Plans (IDPs) as their career evolves.

- A mentee can acquire feedback and gain opportunities to explore, discuss, and test their ideas, strategies, and plans in a friendly forum.

- A mentee can learn how to earn long-term trust, loyalty, confidence, and even friendship of worthy people in their organizations.

In the balance of this book, we will explore how mentoring can be used to each organization's and employee's advantage, and where this management/leadership art appears to be heading. We will at times pay respect to the older forms of mentoring by offering suggestions on how these programs can be made more effective. But this book is unabashedly devoted to promoting the new Information Age mentoring.

Chapter One:
The Renewed Interest
in Mentoring

*M*entoring is one of the oldest forms of human development. The willingness to share special skills and knowledge that a person accumulated through work and from others in their field laid the foundations for the earliest civilizations. Mentoring cannot be considered a fad or an inconsequential activity.

Homer's Mentor was a special type of faithful and beneficent individual. In time, the term "mentor" came to refer to a person who serves as trusted friend, guide, teacher, adviser, and helper to another individual. Today, one widely accepted *definition of mentoring* is:

An exceptional developmental, caring, and sharing relationship where one person invests their time, know-how, and effort in enhancing another person's growth—in insight, perspective, and wisdom as well as knowledge and skill—and responds to other critical needs in the life of that person to prepare them for greater productivity, understanding, or achievement in the future.

Also, a mentor is often described as:

> *... anyone who has a significant, highly memorable, beneficial life-enhancing effect on another person, generally as a result of personal one-on-one voluntary assistance, that is helpful to them in a relationship which goes beyond duty or obligation.*

–from *Mentoring*, Gordon Shea

In some ways, the latter definition is more significant, since it stresses the importance of voluntary action, one of the most important characteristics of mentoring. Mentors also often mentor people who later become mentors themselves, ensuring that key information and practices flow through generations to solidify our culture and civilization.

Mentoring is gaining renewed attention today for a number of reasons. It can provide an inexpensive way to develop an organization's personnel. Often the resources and the customers are already in place within the organization. Mentoring is highly flexible and quickly applied; it is based on meeting the immediate needs of the mentee, and crafted by the mentor based on their existing knowledge, skills, and imagination. Training courses and educational experiences provided by the organization, or garnered in other ways by the participants, often provide the techniques and content for the mentor–mentee transactions.

Active listening and other feedback techniques can be learned in a supervisory or leadership course and used by a mentor for decades in a series of a mentoring relationships. Similarly, a set of problem analysis–decision making skills, learned by a maintenance person in a course to prepare them for cross-training other personnel, can prepare a mentee to successfully adapt a mentor's "knowledge gift" to make it work for him (or her) throughout a career. The mentoring relationship often becomes the "workshop" for developing or trying out new ideas and techniques.

Mentoring can advance *workplace democracy* and the interests of previously denied groups. Prior to the 1970s, organizations often used mentoring to help members of select groups advance in the organization. Today, other groups of employees who were not so favored in the past have declared, "We want in." Women, as well as members of racial, ethnic, and other definable groups, have seized upon mentoring as a way to gain advantages equivalent to those of the previous "old boy network."

Where Industrial Age mentoring programs tended to develop managers and executives who looked, thought, and acted as their elders did, new mentoring programs increasingly draw out the diverse character and abilities of individuals. These new programs are often initiated by the group members themselves. Today's forward-thinking human resources executives tend to support these group efforts. They recognize that women's efforts to break through the glass ceiling and organizational efforts to achieve workplace fairness, workforce diversity, and employee development are beneficial to the whole organization and are often intertwined.

In the 1970s, when the women's movement was in full swing, Frank Gallo (then Director of Training at the Amacom division of Litton Industries) said, "The current trend of women mentoring women to attain advancement into and up the organizational ladder has the potential of doubling the talent and brainpower available to corporate America."

Many programs that are initially developed to meet the needs of special groups often expand to include a broader range of participants.

Mentoring conserves and transfers special know-how. Technical mentoring, as it is often regarded, is frequently used to bring new technical hires up to speed in a short time. This kind of mentoring also enhances product knowledge and smoothes the edges on newly-formed work teams. It can provide an efficient adjunct to apprenticeship and certification training.

Richard Jaffason, Executive Director of the National Certification Commission in Chevy Chase, Maryland, underscores the broader role that mentoring plays in the certification process. As Jaffason points out, "A waste-water plant operator, a process engineer at a food or drug production facility, or a control operator at a hazardous chemical facility must be far more than a competent technician. [These individuals] cannot afford gaps in their understanding of the relationship between what their jobs entail and the broader environment in which their work is performed." A technician's actions have a potential impact on a host of people, places, and things; certification must include developing "a sense of social responsibility." This is where mentoring comes into play. "Mentoring offers special counseling and a variety of forms of support. It aims at developing a well-rounded individual with balanced judgment, broad perspectives, and even a kind of wisdom."

Many companies first began to recognize (in many cases, belatedly) the need to transfer special organization-specific knowledge during the 1980s, when precipitous downsizings produced substantial losses in organizational memory and know-how. More recently, many organizations which offered early retirement incentives discovered that much expertise went out the door with those who departed. In some cases, the companies had to hire such individuals back on a temporary basis to train others.

In an effort to identify effective approaches to downsizing, Michael Hitt and his colleagues at Texas A&M University interviewed executives at 65 companies that had undergone large-scale reductions in workforce. Executives at firms that had managed a relatively smooth transition often identified mentoring as one of several helpful initiatives. These companies maintained mentoring programs prior to and during the actual layoffs. The programs aimed at developing new leadership as well as retaining technical knowledge.

Mentoring encourages mentee contribution. In the past, mentees were almost never seriously trained to take an active role in a mentoring relationship. Junior personnel were commonly paired with very senior people, and were treated as "empty vessels waiting to be filled" by their mentor. Today the emphasis is often on employee participation, worker empowerment, and team decision-making. This belies the notion that lower level employees have little or nothing to contribute aside from doing their assigned tasks. Consequently, mentees are increasingly being trained in how to make the most of being mentored and how to participate as a partner in their own development.

The new mentor-mentee team is more focused on mentee performance, and more proactive in contributing to technical and organizational problem solving than ever before. Central to today's mentoring efforts is the goal of greater mentee involvement and responsibility. This attitude encourages the rapid transfer of technical know-how, creative ideas, and special perspectives, and leads the mentees to more readily accept and use all offered information, as well as to contribute their own ideas and know-how.

There has been a shift in many organizations from relying on position power and management to a greater use of an individual's inner (personal) power and to more democratic leadership practices (such as in creation of self-managed teams).

Mentoring also brings employees together in a new social environment. The shift from management to leadership, the growing employee insistence on participation in decision-making, and the increasing importance of quality-of-work life and workforce diversity issues have created a new social context within progressive organizations.

As one element within this new social context, mentoring appears to liberate a person's innate sense of altruism. In Industrial Age organizations many people were often unwilling to share their knowledge, fearing the recipient would use it to get their jobs or move ahead of them. Others were angry because they had to struggle to gain their own competence and position, and would just as soon let others go through the same difficulty (since they could seldom get even with the person or people who caused them such grief). And still others were so focused on achieving their own goals that they believed helping others interfered. However, today in virtually every organization or community, many unsung heroes (i.e., mentors) are happily helping others to develop their abilities with or without organizational support.

Mentoring can bring individuals together, often for a very long time. It helps individuals get to know one another more closely than in other types of associations. The prevalence of helping, characteristic of mentoring, creates goodwill and even produces friendship between the two individuals. In this way, mentoring is an effective way for organizations to encourage people to derive good feelings about their work, their work-mates, and their workplaces. See the box, "An Example of Mentoring At Its Best" on the following page.

In an increasing number of organizations, the development of a type of "neural network" of mentors and mentees who, because of their trusting contacts throughout the organization, are able to pass information more effectively, directly and quickly from where it is received to where it is most needed.

Current mentoring practices often provide for individuals to have multiple mentors over time, with each one chosen to meet a set of specific needs. For example, one mentor may help an individual master a particular technical field, another may enable that same person to successfully assume a supervisory role, and a third may help him or her learn to manage large projects or programs. As people's lives lengthen and more individuals launch two or three careers during their lives, the number of mentors and/or mentees a person has is likely to increase. Mentoring can help us to create a great many helping relationships and consequently a more civil and caring workplace.

AN EXAMPLE OF MENTORING AT ITS BEST

What makes or breaks an employer-based mentoring program is the commitment demonstrated by leaders, program champions, and the mentors and mentees themselves. Workforce Development, Inc., an employment and training provider serving ten counties in southeast Minnesota, has trained over 1,000 employees representing 350 organizations on how to become effective mentors and/or develop successful mentoring programs. The training was made possible through a grant from the McKnight Foundation. The employers that commited to the process and made an effort to incorporate it into their culture were the ones that benefited most from mentoring.

The program at Saint Elizabeth's Medical Center is a prime example of mentoring at its best. Jim Root, human resources manager, and Rita Fox, vice president long term care, and other key employees at Saint Elizabeth's in Wabasha, Minnesota were looking for a way to retain certified nursing assistants (CNAs) and help them grow and develop in their healthcare careers. The orientation for new CNAs was a short process. "The mindset was: 'Let's get them trained. Let's get them on the floor and get them going!' This wasn't enough," Root said. They formed a team to begin sketching out a mentoring program to meet their needs. They trained trainers to work with their mentors and recruited employees who were good role models (strong performers with a customer focus, positive attitude, and good communication skills) to mentor others. Mentors promised a minimum of one year and received eight hours of training. Every new nursing assistant was assigned a mentor.

At the beginning of the program, turnover among CNAs was around 64 percent. It dropped significantly and stabilized around 20 percent in 2001. Rita Fox believes the improvement in retention can be attributed to the mentoring program. She and Jim Root are extending the mentoring program to licensed practical nurses (LPNs) and mentoring is becoming a way of life at Saint Elizabeth's. They learned it was the culture and not the tasks that the new employees needed help with assimilating.

"Overall, we have more stable staff and our residents have more consistent care. We have higher morale among staff because of increased job satisfaction. I think our program has been very successful. We learned that training was very important. When we tried to go without training, it didn't work. Training mentors is worth that up front time and added expense. If you put it there, you aren't paying it out on the other side all of the time," Fox explained.

The Wilder Research Center published a guide, *How Welfare-to-Work is Working*, in March 2000. Employer-based mentoring is cited as one of the most promising local support services. The report reads: "Workplace mentoring made it less intimidating for those with little job experience to enter the workforce... Advice and support from co-workers, rather than an authority figure, created a non-threatening work environment, which appears to be a promising job retention strategy." Workforce Development, Inc. followed up with several employers in southeast Minnesota who've started mentoring programs. All of the employers point to increased retention and/or greater employee job satisfaction as key benefits.

–Janine Till, Mentor Program Development Coordinator, Workforce Development, Inc.
www.workforcedevelopment.ws

Mentoring helps individuals reach their full potential. It takes a strong and able workforce to create a strong and able organization. On-the-job training and workshops of various sorts can provide employees with most of the knowledge and skills they need to get their jobs done. Tutoring and coaching by supervisors and technical personnel can round off this development. But people often sense there is another, more personal dimension that is not being addressed effectively. They are vaguely aware that something in the way they work or relate to others is thwarting their development—but they cannot define the problem or attack it successfully.

One person may fear speaking up in a crowd; another may be driven by an inner anger; another may be so competitive that he or she cannot adjust to a team program. Still another may not know how to dress appropriately, or how to plan a part-time college program. A mentor may not be able to solve all such problems (or be expected to), but the mentor can listen to the problem, assist in clarifying the issues, help the employee identify a solution, and encourage the mentee's new behavior.

Harvard University professor Howard Gardner and other researchers in the field of human potential are exploring the frontiers of a deeper kind of workforce diversity. Gardner's concept of the "Seven Flavors of Genius" is opening new vistas for mentoring that go beyond just the rational and logical realms that so dominated twentieth century management. Utilizing a wider range of talents and abilities from the organization's brain pool is particularly useful in building high-powered work teams and increasing their versatility. Today mentors are searching for new ways to increase workgroup versatility.

Mentoring can also offer an organization a long-term bottom line advantage. If a mentor strengthens a mentee's character, helps them develop a greater sense of self, or interests them in furthering their education, the gains will not only benefit the individual and their performance, but such inner strength can offer payback for the length of their career. The positive effects pass through to the next generation of employees.

The closeness that mentors and mentees develop permits a type of candor and caring assistance that overcomes past roadblocks and opens new vistas. Many executives and managers recognize that mentoring is an idea whose time has come–again.

Mentoring can assist in successful integration into the emerging global culture. Mentoring has long been a primary device for helping newcomers adapt and blend into the culture in their adopted nation or environment. As a nation of immigrants, the United States has been a prime example of this. Those who came first were often true pioneers who helped succeeding arrivals adjust to their new environment by helping and mentoring these "greenhorns."

Today, with so many American firms and their personnel going global and new immigrants and workers arriving daily, mentoring serves as a two-way street in the adapting process.

This use of mentoring often focuses on subtleties of the new environment whether it is an electrical worker or an executive going abroad, or a knowledge worker (scientist, engineer, or medical practitioner) or student coming into the U.S. In almost all cases they need information, assistance, and guidance that is not written down anywhere. This often involves the intuitive nuances of a relationship to the unstated expectations of one's behavior.

Effective mentoring is being arranged by major corporations for personnel going out of, or coming into our nation. See the Dow Chemical box on page 48.

Mentoring can enhance an organization's competitive position. Usually bottom line considerations are not the primary driving force behind the use of mentoring within organizations, but it often helps. This seems strange in one respect, since mentoring is always purposeful and aims at enabling people to improve their performances, often in a variety of productive ways.

Yet when people speak of their mentors and of the mentoring received, they frequently discuss life- or style-altering effects. They talk about how mentoring improved their skills, gave them insider knowledge, and/or made them more effective. There exists a general recognition that mentoring pays off through improved personal productivity, better decision-making, and enhanced job performance. Though not measurable these things can only help to an organization's bottom line.

However, mentoring is such a personal thing, varying in effect so greatly from person to person, that it is difficult to evaluate the learning progress. The mentor tries to discover the extent of the mentee's knowledge, skills, and abilities and then fill in the gaps with mentor-specific (but also unique) forms of help. Consequently, there is no standardized test to measure or prove the effectiveness of a mentoring relationship. Mentors who have helped numerous mentees report that every relationship is unique. Mentee needs are as diverse as the human beings who present themselves, and the art of the mentor shapes their development in equally unique ways. Mentoring is a treacherous area for those who love to keep scorecards.

The quiet mastery of complex and interrelated behaviors—for example, the honing and polishing of leadership skills—takes considerable time. Since there are no easily discernible increments to learning, the learner's development may be hidden from view until she or he "goes on stage." What the audience sees at that moment appears to be a "whole performance" and a natural outpouring of ability, rather than an act that was long in crafting. The bottom line of that performance is seldom traced to its incrementally acquired origins.

Americans are not known for investing in long-term results. Years may pass between the time a bit of wisdom is passed from mentor to mentee and the occasion for its use arises. Mentors add to their mentees' capabilities, supplying them with the ammunition needed for future struggles. Since such payoffs are in the indefinite future, there is no practical way to factor many of them into the bottom line. And when these events happen, there will be no way to credit them appropriately. We need to take these gains on faith—very much as we do with any investment in educating our young. We know we couldn't maintain our society if we didn't do so, yet we can't add up those effects. It may be years, or even decades, before some ideas develop.

The final scene of Homer's mentoring saga is instructive. Mentor supplies Telemachus, now grown, with the weapons this warrior prince and his father, Odysseus, needs to battle the would-be usurpers of the throne of Ithaca. Even the gods of ancient Greece did not foresee the ultimate consequence of Mentor's help.

Mentoring helps develop a more civil and successful society. The Training and Development Corporation, a not-for-profit organization headquartered in Bucksport, Maine, operated a summer employment program in which disadvantaged young people (ages 14 to 21) worked for ten weeks in a local company. Supported by the U.S. Department of Labor, the program matched each youth with a volunteer supervisor. Participating supervisors completed a mentoring workshop that trained them in how to reach young people who had been unsuccessful in both school and prior job assignments. To date, the program has produced highly rewarding experiences for the supervisor-mentors. Many of the young participants reported a newfound confidence in themselves, and a new hope for their future.

Actually, this type of program is far from unique. Tens of thousands of volunteer mentors are working in their communities, schools, and religious institutions to help young people live better lives, benefit from more varied options, and gain success in critical "gateway" activities. Volunteers in successful "stay in school" programs help high school students gain self-esteem, see themselves as achievers rather than failures, and expand their horizons to include previously unthinkable possibilities. Among these community mentors are FBI field agents, Coast Guard captains, and small businesspeople, as well as carpenters, janitors, and retired school teachers who care about what happens to our young people. The key in many cases is that participation as mentors in many of these programs are employer-sponsored or encouraged.

But regardless of their sponsorship, several important themes tie these programs together. They are one-on-one and very personal; encourage listening, caring, and other forms of involvement between mentors and mentees; and provide a cumulative beneficial effect on mentees that counteracts some of the negative forces at work in society.

A wise mentor said to me a long time ago: "If I have a dollar and you have a dollar and I give you mine and you give me yours, we each still have a dollar. But if you have an idea and I have an idea and I give you my idea and you give me your idea, we now each have two ideas." This is the essence of the synergy provided by the cooperative teams many organizations are developing. Mentoring can greatly enhance movement toward such goals since we are rapidly becoming a knowledge-based society and new thinking is needed.

Imagine a six or seven person customer service team, recently assembled from various organizational units to develop a new service for patrons or a new product, or service, that the organization is developing. Imagine also that each team member has their own network of mentors back in their departments and that the team is to be a self-managed one where decisions are made by consensus.

It may be difficult for many readers to believe that such a democratic model can function effectively. Yet thousands of today's more mature workplaces are functioning this way very successfully, and more are established daily because of the creative and superior results they can, and most often do, produce.

This is no "leaderless group." The leadership passes from person to person depending on who has the best ideas, the greatest knowledge, or the most applicable experience related to the problem at hand. This type of an advanced organizational model requires a high level of training, sophistication, and maturity, but it harnesses most cooperatively and effectively all of the brainpower of the team and their support system.

The point here is to imagine that each member has "a network of mentors" they have worked with before to brainstorm with, bounce their ideas against, and pick up experiences and insights.

It should not be difficult to imagine what an idea-rich environment would exist within the team as each member pooled their resources. Each team member would also, from time to time, mentor their peers and increase the group's pool of available ideas.

Many types of mentoring relationships are developing, and the investment in other people that mentors are making is increasing. As a result, the varied uses of mentoring have piqued the interest and imagination of individuals who see opportunity for personal and organizational gain through the use of this extraordinary form of human development.

CHAPTER TWO:
WHAT MAKES MENTORING
DIFFERENT AND SPECIAL

*M*entoring can serve as developmental catalyst, change facilitator, an employee-linking device, or even an organizational neural network. It can often be an intellectual supplement, an employee retention plan, and a performance builder. But mostly, mentoring is a tool for broadening the vision and capability of virtually every employee. We should also realize that much mentoring is based on informal relationships that management doesn't ever know exist.

In an increasing number of organizations mentoring has become a way to knit the organization together, extend the organization's impact beyond the corporate walls to society at large, and create a healthier, more prosperous business world. Some see mentoring as a highly effective strategy for helping individuals adjust to the rapid changes occurring in their personal lives, their organizations, and society as a whole.

Because organizations tend to institute mentoring formally, many people see the arrival of such a program in terms of past experience with similar efforts-as "just another short-lived fad." Contrary to these perceptions, mentoring is a form of one-on-one training and development; it is one of the three basic ways that we teach and learn.

Exhibit 2-1. Basic Types of Learning.

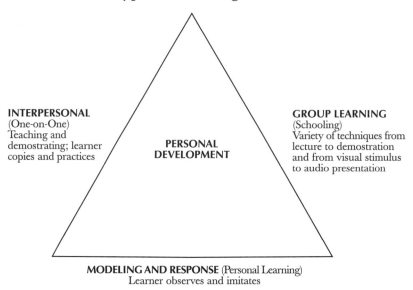

INTERPERSONAL
(One-on-One)
Teaching and
demostrating; learner
copies and practices

PERSONAL
DEVELOPMENT

GROUP LEARNING
(Schooling)
Variety of techniques from
lecture to demostration
and from visual stimulus
to audio presentation

MODELING AND RESPONSE (Personal Learning)
Learner observes and imitates

Modeling and Response. This is the most basic form of teaching and learning, and occurs almost from the time we are born. Our parents communicate with us repetitively, and eventually we learn to mimic their behavior. In time, each of their behaviors enters our own repertoire of behaviors. As we develop, this kind of modeling becomes more abstract. For example, by watching a movie or reading a book, we learn complex ways to behave—e.g., we model styles of leadership based on fictional or historical heroes. Shadowing (often used in mentoring)—where a novice follows a more experienced person around and learns from that role model how to do a job, is one form of modeling and response.

Interpersonal (One-on-One). This form of human development probably began when groups of people had an art, a custom, or a bit of science or technology (such as a knowledge of healing herbs or what pigments to use in cave paintings) they wanted to pass on to talented, gifted, or interested individuals. This preserved the knowledge or skill for the benefit of the group or tribe, and is the essence of most mentoring.

Group Learning (Schooling). Group teaching and learning is a response to the economics of need and the availability of knowledge or skills that can effectively be communicated to many others at one time. This form of group development is also quite old and can be traced back to the emergence from hunting and gathering societies to reasonably fixed communities. It endures because it provides social interaction and cross-learning, in addition to the transfer of large amounts of knowledge and skill to groups of people. It will probably never be completely replaced by solitary learning in front of a computer screen. When the teacher identifies particular talents or interests in individuals and strengthens those abilities, we often get "informal" mentoring.

By taking a closer look at each of these forms of learning, we can put mentoring into its proper perspective and begin to answer the question this chapter raises—what is it that gives mentoring its special power?

ADDING AN EXTRA DIMENSION TO ONE-ON-ONE DEVELOPMENT

A teacher typically imparts bits and pieces of knowledge or skills one step at a time. He or she then helps the learner link each piece of knowledge to other pieces, until a "unit" of learning is achieved. For example, children learning their "ABCs" are taught one letter at a time in the correct order until they can repeat the entire alphabet. Then they put these letters together to form written words.

There are five types of one-on-one learning relationships, and each involves some form of teaching—passing on bits of information (and, to a lesser degree, skills) in long chains until a module of learning occurs. However, there are important differences between these relationships. (A teacher passes on knowledge while a coach may work on the physical performance of the individual, shaping various behaviors and actions into a more productive whole.)

Exhibit 2-2. Modes of One-on-One Teaching and Helping.

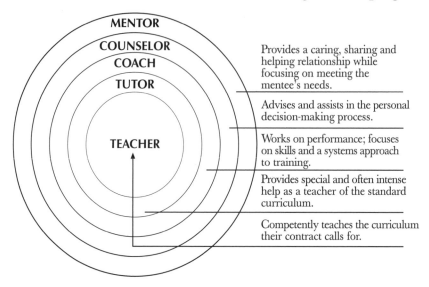

Teacher. A teacher seldom just lectures, especially today. One-on-one interaction abounds in the average classroom, as when a student asks a question or when the teacher calls upon a student to respond. The effect of this teacher-student interaction usually offers learning to the whole class and may even enhance the teacher's awareness, knowledge (by association of a new idea with his or her existing knowledge), or insight.

Tutor. A tutor normally covers the same ground in the same way as a teacher, but on a more one-to-one basis. The closeness of the relationship enables the tutor to detect and close gaps in the learner's knowledge, or to address difficulties the learner is having. The tutor can respond directly to the learner's needs or even experiment with alternate and more effective ways of communicating with that individual.

Coach. One-on-one coaching (as opposed to team coaching) allows the learner to receive specialized attention whenever a problem occurs. The coach pays attention to the details of the total "human system," synchronizing all parts of the individual who is learning the task. For example, in helping someone make an artful presentation, the coach attempts to guide the presenter in crafting a display of him or herself, as well as of the material to be presented, and so achieve the total desired effect.

Counselor. Within organizations, counseling is often seen as a means of improving individual behavior or performance. Used ineptly as an effort to force certain behavior, it can evoke employee coping mechanisms and cause the problem to go underground rather than be resolved. To use counseling constructively, the counselor must focus on helping the individual become successful and productive in the workplace or other environment. When used this way, counseling can produce harmony between the interests of the individual and those of the organization.

Mentor. The distinctive aspect of mentoring is that it focuses almost entirely on meeting the needs of the mentee that the mentor is working with at that moment or time period. The mentor devotes him or herself to this unselfish effort.

A teacher (and members of other professions as well) may operate in any of these five roles. One teacher may just teach. Another may also tutor or coach a given student. Some may counsel, and a few may mentor. Mentoring is a special relationship, and it requires its own set of attitudes, values, and behaviors.

The person most likely to serve in all five relationships to a single individual is most likely to be a parent because of the long and close association with their child. A parent who is willing and able to spend time helping their child develop as fully as possible tends to slide easily from one kind of teaching and helping role to another.

For example, a concerned and effective parent may teach their child the life skills he or she has learned, as well as introduce them to the wider world of learning through reading books to them. He or she may tutor their child while helping them with their homework. As the child grows, coaching and counseling is a natural add-on to the relationship. Finally, with thought and concern the parent might also become a mentor.

MENTORING: AN EXCEPTIONAL EXPERIENCE

Consider the "good, better, best" teachers you had in school. It is likely that during your formal education through high school, you had between 15 and 50 teachers. It is also likely that the majority of these teachers were "good" teachers: they taught their subjects competently, followed the curriculum, and you learned at least enough to move on to the next grade or course level. Teachers like these did their duty and earned their pay. You may have practiced what they taught you until it became part of your daily performance, but the experience of being in their class may be difficult to remember clearly.

Probably, you also had some teachers who offered you more than competence. These "better" teachers invested more in mastering the material and excelling in their presentation of it. They were the teachers who made their subjects come alive. Their classrooms often crackled with energy. They challenged their students, and created imaginings their students had never envisioned before. These teachers were responding to their own inner drive to do the best possible job they could. While this is certainly a valuable and worthy motivation and the results inspiring, it's a self-oriented one. They revel in the favorable feedback they get from their students.

However, if you were especially fortunate, you had one or more teachers who touched your life and influenced it significantly for the better. Such teachers went beyond the curriculum or teaching obligations. They invested time, energy, imagination, and effort in helping you make a life- or style-altering change. These individuals are the people we fondly remember as mentors. These were our best teachers because they reached beyond their material and touched us in a memorable and life-improving way.

Mentors come in all styles and types. They may be patient listeners who permit us to ventilate the strong feelings (anger, fear, or grief) that are keeping us stuck in place. They may be stern taskmasters who hold us to the highest standards of performance we are capable of, even when we do not think we are capable of them. They may be patient encouragers who help us move toward some goal of our own. Or they may be technical or professional people who teach us the ropes, drawing out skills we didn't know we had (or only vaguely recognized) and lighting a spark that caused us to aspire to professional level performance. Yet all of these types of mentors voluntarily make an investment in us that goes beyond their duties and obligations.

The effects of mentoring may occur so slowly and subtly that neither mentor nor mentee is fully aware of the change. The mentor is simply doing what he or she likes to do, wanting only to help the mentee. And the mentee is simply participating in a change process that may take years (and possibly additional mentors) to complete.

At the same time, both mentor and mentee usually gain deeply felt satisfaction from even a short-term mentoring relationship. The following endorsements are representative of the thousands of comments I have received from individuals who have had the experience.

Finally, it is important to realize that any teacher, tutor, coach or counselor can become a mentor, as can any parent, friend, associate, or supervisor, but only a few make the grade. Each such person may do their job adequately, well, or superbly and still not become a mentor.

In a very real sense, the mentee decides which mentors have made an important beneficial impact on their lives. I have been surprised on several occasions when someone who has become very successful, identified me as one of their primary mentors. One was a college president, another director of personnel for a large federal agency, and a third chief executive officer of a major international industrial firm. I remembered the incidents and relationships that led to their conclusion, but I was certainly unaware of the magnitude of the impact.

An Exceptional Experience for Mentees

The following comments come from individuals who participated in a formal six-month mentoring program.

"I never dreamed that I could learn so much in so little time. His insights into the nature of the organization, how it works, and what it rewards, will, I'm sure, make an enormous difference in my career. But it is our friendship that I will value the most."

"When I came to really know her, I knew I'd not feel alone again as long as there were people like her in the organization. I've learned to trust more and to take charge of my own future through her help."

"I couldn't believe that a highly successful executive could care so much about what would happen to me. I hope I can repay him by making good use of all those special insights he provided. All I can say was, 'Thanks for everything!' It doesn't seem like enough."
"I'm contributing much more to our work team effort than I was just six months ago. I've been able to turn my whole attitude around. I'd give him credit for that but he wouldn't accept it. He'd say I did it, he only helped; but without that help I doubt if I'd have made it. The mentoring experience has changed my life for the better."

"Now that I know what mentoring is, I plan to do voluntary mentoring in our community. Helping young people will help pay back what I've gained. Thanks!"

An Exceptional Experience for Mentors

Mentors also report interesting and sometimes surprising responses to their mentoring experiences.

"Mentoring has added another dimension to my leadership skills. Going the extra mile was just an interesting expression until I was trained to function as a mentor."

"I never knew how much was special to me until I began to mentor my technical team members. Things I had observed or reasoned out but never wrote down kept coming back to me as their needs kept popping up."

"During training, getting in touch with my own prior mentoring experiences revealed to me how many valuable things I had gained from the informal mentoring experiences I've had, and how long their effect has lasted—decades in some cases."

"When I help one of my mentees achieve something special and important to them, I feel I've made a powerful investment in our organization's most valuable asset—its people."

"Becoming a mentor helped me stop thinking of my work group as just a group. The very personal one-on-one investment in another person helped me see each one as an individual and then our team as a synergy of harmonies, and as cooperative, unique individuals. I like this."

"Cross-cultural and cross-gender mentoring experiences has opened my eyes, really opened them, to the fresh perspectives, creativity, and dynamic potential inherent in tapping into differences in the work groups.... This is a refreshing change."

Our mentors are the people who helped us change our lives for the better in important ways. You may want to think about the memorable people who stand out from the crowd in your mind. I can also remember three grade school teachers that had a beneficial impact on my writing ability, yet all three were dead before their mentoring bore enough fruit for me to thank them for that mentoring.

If a mentor gives of him or herself, the mentee will almost certainly benefit. Virtually everyone can use encouragement, guidance, information, ideas, new options, and opportunities from time to time. If a mentor notices that an individual has a need, a desire, a hope, an aspiration, a talent, or even a vague discomfort with him or herself, this may be a mentoring opportunity.

Mentoring is seldom a full-time job activity. A teacher will spend most of his or her time teaching, and may also spend time tutoring students who are having trouble with the subject matter. The same teacher may also coach a gifted student for a competitive examination, or counsel him or her about a personal problem. If any of these types of helping go on long enough or are intense enough to make a significant difference in a person's life, that teacher, tutor, coach, or counselor may also become a mentor to that person. Mentoring may take place during odd moments when other students are working on a project or after school hours. Regardless of when it takes place, mentoring is a special form of help that makes a lasting difference.

MENTORING: A VOLUNTARY ACTIVITY

It has been said that you can't hire a mentor. The reason is that a mentor's expectation of compensation could contaminate the relationship. After all, it is difficult to focus exclusively on the needs of the mentee when one's income is involved.

Mentoring adds an extra or special dimension to a helping

relationship, one that is unconditional and as pure as anything in human affairs can be. It is precisely because both participants are free from the burden of duty and obligation that their imaginations can soar. The mentor experiences the unalloyed joy of seeing a friend succeed at his or her chosen goal, and the mentee experiences the joy of achieving that success!

CHAPTER THREE:
MENTORING: A PROGRAM
OR A WAY OF LIFE

*M*any organizations now view mentoring as a flexible developmental art potentially helpful to every member of the workforce. It can be a source of varied opportunities if mentors are trained in using the whole spectrum of mentoring behaviors. Mentoring is a way to enhance the flow of valuable information, skills, insights, and ideas among associates throughout the organization, via any media and in any direction (even from outside the organization).

With a mentee-driven strategy, workers take charge of their own development, are aware of the help available, and seek out situational, informal, and formal mentor training as their needs become more explicit. People can assume either a mentee or mentor role as their needs and abilities dictate for any situation (this is in contrast to the traditional mentor/protégé concept, which implies only a "top down" relationship).

Mentoring is a source of opportunities for diverse supplemental growth experiences, since mentors and mentees can network to maximum effect, and a results-centered (as opposed to process-centered) partnership.

Mentoring is measured by the effect it has on the mentee, now and in the future. A mentor can help an individual turn a corner in his or her life, so from that moment the person is different and behaves differently. Another may help that person master the skills needed to open new doors, build a successful career, live a more satisfying life, and contribute to others more effectively. But the essence of the relationships is that: MENTORS HELP—MENTEES DO! Mentees choose the behaviors they will practice, even though it may take some time. The change must occur in the mentee even if invisible, as with a changed way of thinking.

The benefits of mentoring are not a straight function of the time invested. Mentoring may produce a dramatic change in a moment, or take years of effort to produce a desired outcome. A formal mentoring program, in which mentor and mentee are paired for months, may focus on teaching the basics of a business operation, as the mentor/mentee agreement requires. This produces specific and highly useful results, even though little time is actually spent mentoring in the full sense of the word. The learner's ability to use those basics in more skillful and creative ways may not come until years later. (In organizationally sponsored formal mentoring programs, mentor and mentee typically schedule meetings for one hour or so a week on or off organizational time.)

Mentee involvement must be high. Remember the axiom, Mentors help—Mentees do! Actually, it's not quite that one-sided. The mentor may offer something of value, but the mentee may be unable to make use of that help at that time. This is why empowerment training, as well as a mentee's efforts to overcome a tendency toward passivity, are critical to mentee development. At the same time, mentors may see the mentee's inability to move forward as a problem to be solved—and openly help the mentee confront that problem. This can lead them to cooperatively devise greater, more imaginative efforts.

TYPES OF MENTORING

Exhibit 3-1. Spectrum of mentor interactions.

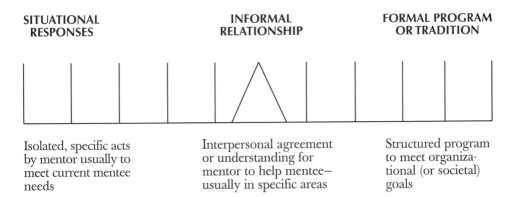

SITUATIONAL RESPONSES	INFORMAL RELATIONSHIP	FORMAL PROGRAM OR TRADITION
Isolated, specific acts by mentor usually to meet current mentee needs	Interpersonal agreement or understanding for mentor to help mentee— usually in specific areas	Structured program to meet organizational (or societal) goals

The characteristics of the three primary types of a mentoring relationship develop along the spectrum of interactions from situational, informal, to formal. These three types blend with one another. Formal mentoring programs can range from tight, bureaucratically controlled operations at the extreme right of the spectrum, to loose associations where the only formal aspect is that the partners agree to meet weekly or decide upon one or more objectives within a general time frame.

Situational Mentoring. Some of the most powerful mentoring experiences occur in short bursts, when an individual provides the right information or ideas at the right moment in another person's life. The mentor may simply be responding to the mentee's need without realizing the impact her or his words are having. In fact, neither party may recognize the activity as mentoring. However, the incident may produce a significant effect on the other person and only later be recognized as powerful mentoring.

The value of such a casual transfer of information or ideas depends largely on how well the mentee accepts and uses the information. If the information offered fits the mentee's needs,

41

the impact can be substantial. Consider the following questions based on your own life experience.

 • Who provided you with an "Aha!" experience that enabled you to grasp the significance of something important—something that had, up until then, eluded you?

 • Who provided you with a "quotable quote" that illuminated the essence of something that suddenly had great meaning for you, so that you still repeat it—even to others?

 • Who helped you discover an ability or talent of yours that had been previously dormant?

When groups of prospective mentors have been asked these three questions, virtually all of them can identify one or more significant person and/or incident that powerfully influenced their lives.

Informal Relationships. Informal mentoring is probably the most common type of mentoring and the relationship may last from a few weeks to a lifetime. Such informal mentoring may lead to friendships that include occasional mentoring experiences for a long time.

Flexible, informal relationships are usually mentor initiated or driven, in that the mentor voluntarily shares whatever expertise or special insights she or he possesses when another person has a need for, or could benefit considerably from such help. While each partner usually has a clearly defined role (giver versus receiver), a peer relationship may develop in which the two switch roles, depending on who needs help at a given time.

When a teacher, tutor, coach, or counselor goes beyond his or her obligations or narrow self-interest, the informal mentoring role often comes into play. This "above and beyond" concept is at the core of much biography and literature (such as many sports epics), in which the helping agent breaks free from the hold of his or her own job obligations and potential gain, and instead does what is best for the mentee. Such individuals are mentors in the full sense of the word.

If you can identify one or more people who were mentors in your life, chances are good that the relationship fit the definition of "informal mentoring." In other words, the relationship carried beyond situational incidents but was not formalized beyond the help given to you—there was usually no stated agreement, official sanction, or established time frame. Exceptional teachers, coaches, supervisors, friends, or a parent may have filled this role with you.

Some organizations train all of their employees to mentor one another informally as needs arise. Surveys in such companies indicate a substantial increase (often 200 to 300 percent) in the number of informal mentoring relationships. There was also a much higher incidence of *situational* mentoring reported by both mentors and mentees. (It was difficult, however, to obtain any statistics comparing the amount of *situational* mentoring that occurred before training and after training, since these episodes were considered "incidental.")

The companies reported a far greater awareness of the availability of mentors and the needs of others for mentoring. People were more sensitive to non-explicit verbal and nonverbal pleas for assistance and other indications that an associate might be experiencing a need or a problem. There was a more effective response to individuals who needed help, since employees were trained to avoid certain non-productive behaviors and to use more effective techniques.

Many organizations also offer training in informal mentoring to those not engaged in an employer-sanctioned formal program.

Formal programs. The goals of some formal mentoring tend to be focused narrowly, so that the mentoring programs are considered for detailed planning, measurement, and evaluation of phenomena, such as the program's impact on company retention rates. By contrast, at the point where the formal and informal models meet, "programs" can be virtually self-managed by the mentor and mentee, and driven by a mutually developed set of objectives. Typically, after employees are trained in both how to mentor and how to be an effective mentee, a mentoring coordinator often determines who in the organization wants to learn or develop specific skills, and who has the appropriate ability to help. He or she will then suggest possible matches, although the participants usually decide whether or not to work together.

Formal mentoring programs can range from light, inexpensive systems to quite burdensome, expensive, and/or heavily managed activities. Deciding which way to go is not always easy. An organization trying to achieve critical changes in the composition of its workforce may want a more structured approach so that it can measure its progress. On the other hand, an organization that wants to speed problem solving, adapt to rapid change, and become as competitive as possible may opt for the self-managed approach.

The four appendices of this book expand on how to maximize results from each of these three types of mentoring as well as how to develop a pilot formal mentoring program.

A Mentoring Analogy

Some people think if they volunteer to serve as a mentor they automatically become one when they begin to work with a mentee. That may or may not be the case. It depends not on the presumed relationship, but on what the mentor does and how the mentee uses the help.

The relationship can be compared to what the broadcast industry calls the "carrier wave." Each radio or television station sends out a general signal on a particular frequency to their broadcast area. This would be comparable to a tutor helping a child review and better understand a math homework assignment-a valuable activity in itself. Like the carrier wave from the station, nothing would happen without that relationship.

However, the radio or television station also "modulates" that carrier wave so that music and pictures as well as other sounds and sensations are available to their audience. This is the content or programming the broadcaster offers. The tutor can offer encouragement and emotional support to the child they are helping, and organize his or her assistance to better match the learning style to the personality of the student. They may even go out of their way to get special help (perhaps an eye exam and glasses) for a student encountering difficulties in their reading. Such a student may regard the tutor as one of their mentors.

However, the mentee is the one who turns the set on or off and chooses the channels they want to tune to. The art of mentoring is providing enough desirable content to influence the mentee's selection from all of the available material.

As our mentees surf the channels of their lives, how can we get them to pause, think, and consider the messages we are broadcasting? If we are successful perhaps they will stay with us for a while.

Thinking as a mentor even when not actively mentoring can be a good thing. It serves as a frequent reminder of why we are in this type of relationship. Well-trained mentors and mentees tend to participate in mentoring relationships as a natural and ongoing part of life. Throughout their careers, and sometimes for decades afterwards, the joy and satisfaction gained from helping or being helped encourages both to serve in either role as the need and opportunity arises. Training mentors and mentees across the entire spectrum of relationships (from situational to formal) enables them to respond more appropriately to the subtleties of a mentee's needs.

Characteristics of Different Types of Mentoring

SITUATIONAL MENTORING ACTS:

Tend to be;
- Short-isolated episodes
- Spontaneous- "off-the-cuff" interventions
- "Seemingly" random
- Often casual
- Creative-innovative

Are generally characterized by being;
- Responsive to current need of Mentee and/or present situation
- A mentor initiated intervention
- "One time" events
- The mentee's responsibility to recognize and use lessons offered
- Unclear as to results at time of incident

May include;
- Sharp, beneficial life or style altering effects on Mentee
- Increased sensitivity of Mentee to *opportunities*
- A network of mentors to be called upon as needed
- Later assessment of results by Mentee

INFORMAL MENTORING RELATIONSHIPS:

Tend to be;
- Voluntary
- Very personal
- Very responsive to Mentee needs
- Loosely structured
- Flexible

Are generally characterized by being;
- Mentor driven by his or her caring, sharing and helping
- Mutual acceptance of roles (giver-receiver)
- A path to developing deep mutual respect and friendship
- Dependent on Mentor's competence, knowledge, skills and abilities

May include;
- Mentee revealed needs
- Periodic assessment of results by participants
- Team mentoring-but with emphasis on intense one-on-one interaction during team activity
- Mentor having more than just a role relationship with mentee- i.e., as a supervisor, parent, teacher, or friend

FORMAL MENTORING PROGRAMS:

Tend to be;
- Measurably productive-long term
- The source of a developing relationship-friendship
- Systematic-structured
- Institutionalized, on-going
- Traditional

Are generally characterized by being;
- Driven by organizational needs
- Focused on achieving organizational or sub-unit goals
- A method for matching mentors with (or assigned to) mentees
- Of fixed duration-based on goal achievement
- Organizationally sponsored or sanctioned

May include;
- Monitoring of program activities
- Measurement of program results, as with organizational change or the advancement of specific groups of mentee
- A focus on goals of a special group
- Specially designed organizational interventions

MENTORING AS A WAY OF LIFE

One of the most cogent arguments for quality mentor and mentee training, employer-sponsored formal programs of reasonable length, and an employer's enthusiastic support for a mentoring effort is that the people so involved are more likely to continue to mentor a variety of associates for the balance of their careers, and their lifetimes.

Some people, because of their temperament, personality, or desire to do well, take to mentoring quite naturally. They mentor from time to time as a likely candidate appears on the scene or a suitable situation arises. Such people often start the process early in life and continue it as long as they are able. It becomes part of their lifestyle.

However, we have also found that many more people are attracted to such an activity, but lack the self-confidence, skills, or the perceived opportunity to assume the role. If such individuals are encouraged to serve as a mentor (or mentee), learn what actually constitutes mentoring, and are trained in ways to competently perform the activity, they will gladly give it a try.

If they enjoy peer support, find the activity satisfying and rewarding, and achieve success in their efforts, they also tend to assume the mantle as a way of life, or as an important part of their life.

Virtually any organization can achieve a mentor-rich organizational culture where people throughout the organization share ideas and information and together develop elegant solutions to the problems and challenges they encounter.

"Mentoring—A Way of Life at Dow"
By Frank T. Morgan, Ph.D.
Global Director Executive Development and Leadership

The tag line we use for mentoring at Dow Chemical Co. is still a touch asprational. We aren't there, yet; but we are making significant progress. The mentoring concept at Dow has received the enthusiastic support of senior corporate and business management, the human resources function, and the employees around the globe who have experienced the benefits of a mentoring relationship.

Dow is a global company with 50,000 employees operating in over 170 countries located around the world (about 30% of the total are in the USA). Mentoring, therefore, has to be more than "a walk down the hall for a chat". It's a long walk from Midland, Michigan to Manila, Philippines, hence, the mentoring processes and tools need to be global, virtual and available across time zones. To accomplish this, Dow's partnership with Triple Creek Associates created an on-line mentoring site that includes data bases, matching capabilities, mentor training, and a solid grounding in Dow's global competencies and effective mentoring principles. This website now provides an effective tool kit.

The right global tools help, but leader support and meeting employee needs are also necessary if mentoring is to become-a way of life. A recent study of the top leaders at Dow identified mentoring as one of the three key events in their personal leadership journey. In addition, the company's People Strategy, launched in 2002, identified mentoring as an important benchmarked practice that would move Dow into world class leadership practices. Thus the support by and accountability for leaders and mentoring is actually present in Dow's culture.

Finally, people engage in activities that they see as important and that meet their needs. For those of us who have had the good fortune of having mentors, the benefits are evident. For those of us who have had the opportunity to mentor others, our satisfaction is clear. Mentoring does, in fact, meet the needs of the firm, the mentors and those on the receiving end of the relationship.

To make mentoring a way of life at Dow, we need to continue to:
- provide global tools
- have leaders actively support mentoring
- measure its effectiveness
- satisfy the needs of all parties in the mentoring relationship

We will get there, and Mentoring will truly become A Way of Life at Dow!

Chapter Four:
The Effective Mentor

*M*entoring is a matter of communicating useful knowledge, ideas, and skills to someone who wants to learn. That sounds simple enough. But as anyone familiar with the study of interpersonal communications knows, some communication behaviors can be very productive–others much less so. Examining these behaviors can help you appreciate some of the more subtle aspects of mentoring.

Behaviors to Avoid

In the past, giving advice, sponsoring, and even "rescuing" (helping the mentee extricate him or herself from a potential calamity) might have been considered the essence of mentoring. We now know these behaviors have a downside–they do little to support a relationship aimed at empowering the learner. Let's take a closer look at the dynamics involved.

Giving Advice

In a mentoring relationship, giving advice shifts responsibility for making a decision from mentee to mentor and curtails personal growth. If the mentee accepts the advice and applies it successfully, the mentor has encouraged dependency. The mentee may return time and again to let the mentor solve his or her problems.

Giving advice often carries a subliminal message of, "You are not able to solve your problem ... let me do it for you." This is why people often resist advice. Rather than be told what to do, they want someone to listen and to support them in their problem solving and decision-making endeavors.

Criticism

Researchers agree there is no such thing as "constructive criticism," no matter how helpful the giver's intent. By definition, criticism is judgmental and usually perceived as threatening. People tend to resist listening to criticism, as well they should. Our most basic needs are for survival and security, and criticism threatens these basics. On the other hand, accepting criticism lowers self-esteem and may lead to lower effectiveness.

Mentees often need someone to help them explore where a course of action may lead and define the gap between what is and what is needed. Factual information concerning the situation can also be beneficial. Explorations such as these encourage personal growth and maturity.

Rescuing

Mistakes can lead to growth, assuming the person recognizes the causes of the mistake and uses that information to make better decisions in the future. But let's be truthful: people seldom learn from their mistakes. If they really did, we should encourage them to make more and bigger mistakes as a "fast track" way of learning.

The issue here is the pattern of one's mistakes. If a person's mistakes are driven by a repetitive pattern, such as driving too fast, skirting the edges of the law, or taking excessive risks in other fields, rescuing them from their folly will encourage them to push the envelope further. Parents who constantly rescue their children from the consequences of their negative or il-conceived acts are the best-known example of this syndrome. They postpone the reckoning—usually disastrous for both when it comes. Ironically, the more the mentor likes a mentee, the more prone he or she may be to rescue the mentee inappropriately.

Sponsoring

In Industrial Age mentoring, it was common for mentors to promote the careers of their "protégés." They became press agents for their young charges, often without regard for the protégé's talent or merit relative to those of others. It was like rooting for the home team, simply because it was theirs.

It is certainly appropriate for a mentor to open a door for a mentee who shows special talent or ability. It's also appropriate to inform the mentee of an opportunity or to help her or him prepare for a desired position. But to invest one's own ego in special treatment for a mentee over others can be the rawest form of favoritism. In a truly fair and competitive arena, relative talent will win out.

Building Barriers

Mentors sometimes build barriers between themselves and their mentees without intending to, and without being aware they are doing so. When lower-level personnel (interns or even supervisors) find themselves paired with executives, they may find the situation flattering—but also scary. Behavior appropriate for the boardroom can be intimidating for someone who needs a relaxed, friendly environment in which to ask questions or take risks.

Ignoring the Why

The essence of training is skill acquisition; its measure is performance. The essence of education is understanding; its measure is new or improved decisions or applications of knowledge and ideas. Many mentors are good at knowing what to do and how to do it and in displaying their skills: their own performance is often measured by how well they do things. Consequently, they may not invest equal time in educating another person. Education takes longer and is more complicated and deals with explaining the why of things so the mentee better understands the reality of what they encounter.

"Reasons why" are at the center of making sense of things in the world of work. Children start asking "Why?" out of curiosity, but may pursue doing so out of a perverse sense that they can drive their parents (who, in the child's opinion, should know everything) nuts with enough "whys." Mentors should be able to admit when they don't know the why of something. This admission can become the cue for a joint exploration of an important issue or a problem-solving exercise. Knowing where to get the answer can be valuable to a mentee who needs to fit knowledge and understanding together in new patterns. Little improvement in an organization can be made without asking why something has been done a particular way and what can be done to improve it.

Discounting

To discount is to put down or make less of someone, something, or themselves as an unconscious way of dealing with their negative feelings about those things or people. For example, we may put ourselves down when we make a mistake ("There I go again.... I never do anything right"), instead of getting on with making it right. Discounting aspects of ourselves or of others is based on a negative assumption without the careful or even conscious assessment of reality. It is all too often based on a false assumption that has not been checked out.

In mentoring, we might discount a mentee's interest, ability, or willingness to do something we think beneficial ("He should take on this project, but he'll probably mess it up."). A mentor's heightened awareness of his or her hesitations and negative assessments can lead to candid discussion. This is risky—but it's a risk that the mentor needs to be open to.

BEHAVIORS TO PRACTICE

Sometimes it seems easier to get someone to practice a positive behavior than to give up a negative one. For example, we can remind ourselves to listen more intently to the concerns of a mentee—a positive behavior. But stifling the urge to give advice can be much more difficult. Positive behaviors are more rewarding, but the negative ones are all too familiar and habitual. Below are some helpful behaviors mentors need to master.

Listening

When a mentee has a concern or problem to discuss, acting as a sounding board may be all that is needed to help this person work through a problem and reach a decision. Careful listening helps mentees maintain ownership of their problem and their decision about how to solve it, and they gain the pleasure and pride of having solved the problem themselves. By listening, the mentor helps an individual become a more efficient problem solver. Often we only need to work through, or get in touch with our negative "feelings" about a problem we have, to clear our minds enough to develop a solution.

Feedback

When someone explains a problem they face, the problem description almost always contains both *facts* and *feelings*. Negative feelings can interfere with a person's problem-solving ability. By giving feedback on the whole message—both the facts and the feelings—you let the other person know that you not only heard them, but understood them. This makes a mentee feel he or she is not alone with this problem. By gaining perspective on the whole problem (the facts and their feelings about those facts), the mentee is more able to dissipate their negative feelings and get on with solving the problem.

Many people "discount" feelings as not being very important or as impediments to problem-solving. The expression "leave your feelings at home" indicates that we are only interested in employing partial people. However, motivation is primarily a matter of feelings, and good or bad feelings lead to a person doing productive or unproductive things. So, since feelings lead to behaviors—take your choice.

How we feel about an event may be more of a problem than the consequences of the event itself. For example, the resentment one feels about being passed over for a promotion can cause someone to hold a grudge—where not getting a promotion only maintains the status quo. This notion may be hard to accept, but it is our feelings that keep us from getting on with our lives. This doesn't mean that we should deny our feelings—they are real and need to be dealt with effectively.

Providing Information and Ideas

Much of what mentors offer a mentee is in the form of information: personal insight, options, and the like. When this information is offered is important. If a person is locked in the throes of a difficult problem, objective data will seem irrelevant— and it often is. However, if the person is able to work through the personal pain, fears, or anger, a time will come where knowledge is helpful. When that time comes, the mentee is ready for decision-making.

Helping a mentee solve a difficult problem or make a critical decision comes in three parts. First, the mentor listens while the mentee talks through the issue. Second, the mentor recognizes the feeling part of the transaction and feeds that back to the mentee to help them clarify their emotional difficulties and move forward. Third, as the mentee's emotional blocks subside, they become more open and in greater need of information, techniques, and ideas with which they can solve the problem or make the decision. At that point if you have any useful, relevant ideas or information, give it.

Context Shifting

Individuals have often been trained to imagine themselves living out a certain role or way of life. These self-images may be outdated, limiting, and even inapplicable. Helping a person (without arguing) see him or herself in a broader, more self-actualizing, and more rewarding light can be a great service. This context must jibe with the mentee's nature and abilities (rather than the mentor's goals for the mentee). But such a shift in self-image can help individuals maximize their potential.

Confrontation

Confronting a mentee's behavior and/or intentions without damaging the mentee's self-image or the relationship is a high art. If the need for confrontation arises, think in terms of giving a clear, non-judgmental description of what you believe the mentee is doing (or intends to do). Describe the negative consequences you anticipate or observe, and express how you feel about that behavior. This should be enough. Hold back any impulse to tell the mentee how to behave or how you would solve the problem. (If we don't give the mentee a directive, there is nothing he or she can argue about or reject.) An artful confrontation gives the mentee something to think about and will usually lead to a constructive decision: one that the mentee will own and hopefully feel good about.

Giving Permission and Offering Encouragement

Before a person can make an important behavior change, he or she may need "psychological permission" from an authority figure, often their mentor, if they trust her or him. The complexities of human behavior are often rooted in early life experiences, parental programming, and notions derived from our culture, training, or economic circumstances. Change is not easy. The person may need to explore the sources of certain behavior patterns and evaluate the consequences of keeping the old behaviors or changing. If the person decides that the change would be good, encouragement and support from a mentor can be critical to his or her success.

Exploring Options

One of the most valuable services a mentor can render is to help a mentee brainstorm or otherwise articulate a variety of options to any decision. These options may be serious or playful, innovative or traditional. Not only does the brainstorming suggest more choices, but it also leads the mentee to more creative variations and a broader perspective on the problem. (Mentoring skills discussed above are explored to greater depth in *Mentoring—How to Develop Successful Mentor Behaviors* [Menlo Park, CA: Crisp Publications, 2001].)

WHAT MENTORS DO

If an organization's leaders view mentoring as a way of life rather than just as a program, then workforce development will be widespread and constant. Mentors trained to use the entire spectrum of mentoring interactions (from situational to formal interventions) can help their associates at all levels whenever the need or opportunity arises, with or without any long-term agreement.

Mentors are people who have special or memorably helpful effects on us and in our lives. Typically, mentors make important contributions to:
- Technical competence

- Character
- Knowledge of how to get things done in or through the organization
- Mental and physical health and fitness
- Understanding of other people and their viewpoints
- Knowledge of how to behave in unfamiliar social situations
- Insights into cultural differences
- Understanding of the historical origins of events and the meaning of specific trends
- Creation of an insightful personal data bank
- Development of values

Good mentors know the value of their time and recognize the need to get their regular jobs accomplished. Consequently, they will set aside a specific interval for regular meetings with their mentees, knowing it takes time to develop a trusting, productive relationship.

Training mentors to perform the range of mentoring activities productively takes time and investment, but the payoffs are reflected in the long-term accomplishments of their mentees and in the fact that the mentor can continue to provide effective mentoring throughout his or her entire career.

"What Can I Contribute?"

Since the older model of top-down (senior to junior) mentoring is giving way to more democratic partnership type of relationships which includes mentoring by peer specialists, more people are finding the idea of mentoring attractive and personally promising. Nevertheless, many prospective mentors are unsure of whether they have anything of value to offer another person. There are several ways to relieve that concern. First, the potential mentor should forego all modesty and ask him or herself: What am I good at? What special experience have I had? When have people asked my help? What things do I encounter that other people need to know about? What kinds of things have my mentors offered me? What would I enjoy helping someone with the most? What would I like to learn that I could use to help others?

After answering such questions as these, the prospective mentor might choose several items to explore more deeply.

EXAMPLES OF MENTOR RELATIONSHIPS

The goals of the mentoring relationship shape the role the mentor will play. Below are three examples of common helping relationships that transcend common workplace associations because of the mentor's focus on the mentee's development. Dozens of other models are possible, depending on the abilities of the mentor and the needs and response of the mentee.

The Role Model demonstrates appropriate attitudes behaviors, protocols, and responses and explains why these are appropriate. They model effective behavior in his or her daily life and within the organization, and inspire the mentee to meet and possibly exceed his or her chosen goals. The role model also demonstrates adaptive behaviors and personal learning and growth and supports and encourages mentee learning and constructive development on an ongoing basis.

The Career Counselor (this is a mentoring role, not the job function of the same name) acts as a sounding board as the mentee sorts through and reacts to the dilemmas of developing their personal career choices. They provides insights into the organization's markets, environment, culture, and values, as well as to evolving changes in any of these areas. The career counselor provides access to sources of career information or acts as a reference guide for paths the mentee may choose and shares their own personal or business contacts to help the mentee gain realistic information on his or her options. They can assist the mentee in planning special career moves, such as lateral moves, assignments on task forces or special projects, and participation in advanced education and training courses. They can also suggest tactics and strategies for accomplishing work objectives, and provide support when the mentee is experiencing stress and uncertainty. The career counselor offers ideas and information on career development materials, resource contacts, and paths to explore in setting up the next stage of the mentee's career path, and shares information and ideas on the evolution of certain careers in a modern context.

The Leadership Coach (note: managers today are shifting their focus to leadership rather than to just managing) offers instructive parables, stories, biographical incidents, and legends about leadership and its responsibilities, and counsels the "whole person" about values, integrity, and ethical conduct when appropriate. They explore issues with the mentee, discussing where certain paths of conduct will ultimately lead, and provide exposure to the values of moral leaders through various media, such as the discussion of films, books, and news stories. The leadership coach helps the mentee recognize outcomes of his or her actions and plans, and acts as foil and friend when engaged in discussions of ethical conduct.

Mentor Responsibilities

To ensure productive relationships with their mentees, mentors take a number of actions. They set realistic expectations for the relationship, for mentee achievement, and their own involvement. The mentor is available—to as great an extent as possible—whenever the mentee has a need. They maintain consistent contact with the mentee to help the relationship develop, listen with empathy, are open minded to the mentee's needs and opinions, and provide encouragement. The mentor must make a conscious effort to build the relationship by following through on commitments, providing emotional support when needed, and frequent communication. They should alert their mentee to existing or developing opportunities that will help the mentee explore options, share information on one's own successes and failures as appropriate, and give and receive constructive feedback when needed.

THE CONSTANTLY DEVELOPING SELF

In the past, organizational mentors tended to develop themselves slowly, if at all, for the mentoring role. This was because their organizations changed slowly, and since they often passed on well-established principles or facts gleaned from their on-the-job experience, not much self-development was considered necessary.

However, with the advent of the "learning organization" and the emphasis on continuously developing everyone within it (i.e., lifetime learning), more mentors are struggling to keep up with—let alone keep ahead of—their mentees. This need not be a problem since a bracing dialogue between mentor and mentee can prove productive and generate mutual learning. If both partners are growing, any concern about who is mentoring and who is being mentored may not be important.

Mentors who make a conscious investment in their own development become a more valuable resource to their organizations and to others.

CHAPTER FIVE:
THE PROACTIVE AND PRODUCTIVE MENTEE

THE EXTRA MILE

*W*hen the armies of Rome occupied the Holy Land in Biblical times, a law stated that any Roman soldier could impress any Jewish youth to carry his armor for one mile. One such soldier began to tell the youth carrying his armor about the places he visited, the things he had done, and some of his adventures. As they walked and talked, the youth carried the armor beyond the required point. When the soldier mentioned that further service was unnecessary, the youth, who had found the soldier's tale fascinating and exciting, replied, "The last mile was for you–this mile is for me."

The story of the extra mile means making an investment in oneself, seeking personal growth, and becoming excited by the world around us. If employee passivity is to diminish and involvement, commitment, and contribution are to replace it, we should more closely analyze the purpose of this extra mile story and our interpretation of it. Mentoring also includes self-investment.

PREPARING TO BE MENTORED

The role of the mentor in the relationship is focused on so intently that an essential point may be forgotten. The reason for mentoring is to help the mentee increase his or her personal effectiveness, knowledge, and productivity. Very few organizations that support ongoing mentoring provide significant training for mentees in "how to make the most of being mentored." (See *Making the Most of Being Mentored—How to Grow From a Mentoring Partnership* [Menlo Park, CA: Crisp Publications, 1999]).

Consider the case of the Freddie Mac Corporation. In 1993, this firm conducted a series of interviews with junior level mentees from the management information systems division who had been paired with company executives for one year in a previous program. While two-thirds of the mentees said their experience had been an unalloyed success and they had experienced considerable growth and development, one-third experienced relationship problems that diminished their gains.

Some of these problems stemmed from mutual shortcomings: neither the mentee nor the mentor fully appreciated the subtleties inherent in the relationship. However, most problems arose because the mentees were passive or held their mentor in such awe that they were unable to relate effectively. Even when the mentees were able to work through these problems, several months had passed during which mentees were reticent or fearful of making a mistake "in the presence of such a high ranking person." The company subsequently modified mentor and mentee training to include discussion on how to recognize and overcome the "awe factor."

Many formal mentoring programs begin the relationship with virtually no mentee training, or even a social-hour orientation session as a "get-acquainted" activity. If the gains of mentoring are to be realized, mentees need to be prepared for the experience. This preparation needs to be well integrated with the organization's overall training plan.

THE POWER ISSUE

Much of the history of mentoring is associated with the notion that mentors were older, wiser, more experienced, and more knowledgeable than their mentees. It often comes as a shock when this notion is challenged. Many people still perceive the mentor-mentee relationship as a kind of parent-child bond. However today, quite a few mentees better educated, more "worldly-wise," and more technically competent than their mentors. It's unwise to view mentees on the basis of assumptions or stereotypes.

For example, executives at fairly high levels have often climbed the corporate ladder by excelling in a narrow specialty—such as engineering or accounting—and by managing people in that specialty. They may have spent their whole careers in one firm or one kind of business and failed to learn much about related technological developments, such as computer-based information management systems. By contrast, their mentees may be broadly educated and well trained, may have advanced in several organizations, and had overseas assignments, as well as mastered recent technology.

One dramatic example of this age inversion was related by Jack Welch, now retired chief executive officer of the General Electric Corporation. At one point he began to feel "behind the curve" in learning to use computers, appreciating the potential of the internet, and understanding the implications inherent in the dot coms. In his book, *Jack—Straight from the Gut* (New York, NY: Warner Books, 2001), he tells a great story, with a surprise twist, about a business trip to London in 1999. Welch met a 36-year-old executive of GE unit in London who mentioned, during a meeting, that "he had just met with his mentor." Welch was curious and asked how the executive came to have a mentor and why the mentoring wasn't aimed at the people who would normally be expected to be in such a program. That is when the executive explained that he and a 23-year-old were spending three to four hours a week teaching him how to use the Internet—*the executive was the mentee.* Welch immediately was taken with the idea, especially to find that a guy that young was using an even younger person as a mentor. When Welch returned home he immediately asked his top 500 leaders to get Internet mentors, "preferably under the age of 30." The mentors, many of them less than half the age of the executives, worked with these leaders for three to fours hours a week. He later explained the program to the top 3,000 managers in the company. It was a great way to turn the company upside down. In the end Welch said that the benefits proved to be even greater—during these Internet learning sessions many causal conversations managers were also discovering new talent, and gaining a better understanding of what was really going on in the company.

Even the most sophisticated mentees can still learn a lot from internal senior personnel. In such situations, the mentor may begin the relationship by acquainting their mentee with the peculiarities of the organization's business, evolving corporate culture, efforts being made to capture new markets, and dozens of other points that could help the mentee operate effectively in their new organization.

The Industrial Age mentoring model assumes that mentees will eventually achieve "position power"—the power that comes from holding a particular job at an exalted level. While this may still be important in some organizations, the development of expert power and inner power (the power that comes from mental agility, creativity, persuasiveness, energy, stamina, determination, vision, and problem solving) are increasingly potent in mentoring for the Information Age.

Mentoring is increasingly seen as a partnership. Mentees are expected to play an active role in their development by identifying their own needs (to as great an extent as possible), making those needs specific, soliciting mentor assistance, and making effective use of that help to benefit both the organization and themselves.

THE MENTOR-MENTEE PARTNERSHIP

Defining the mentoring relationship as a partnership makes it clear that each participant has a role, and mutual investment is required to attain mutual gain. Formal mentoring programs that are driven by the mentee, as opposed to the mentor, ensure that participation is voluntary on both sides. It also lowers the risk of Equal Employment Opportunity legal problems. These can be based on some mentees finding, more powerful and influential mentors than other participants in a formal mentoring program. Problems can occur here there is the potential for advancement implied—such as with an intern program.

What benefits can the mentee expect from a formal mentoring partnership? Even the most sophisticated mentees can benefit from the opportunity to learn from the mentor's particular experiences, personal insights, knowledge, and know-how. It's a chance to test their own ideas, tactics, and strategies in a friendly forum, and provides inside knowledge of the organization's culture, political structure, and vision. Through the mentor relationship, the mentee can develop a network of contacts (technical, administrative, and organizational leaders) to keep them abreast of important organizational changes, and have insight into the specific behaviors that support organizational goals and actions. This relationship will help the mentee in defining their personal career and other developmental objectives, and thereby expose them to the experiences of a mentor in other functional areas of the organization and consequent personal development. It will also give them access to special mentor-designed learning experiences, as well as coaching and counseling.

Informal mentor-mentee relationships, by contrast, are more likely to focus on specific areas of mentor expertise, specific mentee needs, or areas of common interest that bring the two individuals together.

As for situational mentoring, this is most often designed by the mentor to achieve a specific and usually lasting result. It is often a short-term intervention often delivered with dramatic effect and is creatively or incisively constructed. For most people, situational mentoring is the hardest to appreciate because it is episodic. There may or may not be an ongoing relationship so that association (if any) may not involve any further mentoring. Often it is a "one shot" assistance.

The essence of being in a mentee role is a need and/or desire for help. Open, effective, two-way communication (along with a bit of humor) is the medium for finding a way to achieve one's maximum productivity, career success, and empowerment.

GETTING TO KNOW YOURSELF AND OTHERS

"If it's to be, it's up to me," might well be the daily mantra for the proactive mentee—the person that takes charge of their life and makes the most of it. However, that is not as simple as it sounds. One of the greatest gains for humanity in the twentieth century was the advances in our understanding of our selves, those around us, and how and why we interact as we do. The findings of researchers and observers of the human condition in the social, psychological, and communications sciences are of inestimable value to the mentee who wants to develop a satisfying, rewarding, and even joyful career (and personal life).

It is easy to assert that each human being is unique (which they are), yet how does a person define their uniqueness and develop their strengths to the fullest? It's not easy. Yet only by finding out who we are—deep down inside—will we seek out the mentors we need to make the most of our lives.

Mr. Dyke—An Example of Situational Mentoring

I was raised in a "working class" neighborhood that I saw as having a culture of resistance to authority. I developed a "goof off" attitude and wanted to get as much from a situation as I could and give as little of myself as possible.

Yet I was ambitious in my own way and had aspirations. The one thing I really enjoyed as a teenager was the camping and outdoor activities offered through the Boy Scouts. Each year our troop had a contest based on rank advancement, the merit badges earned, attendance, and other factors. The three or four winners were taken on a trip to climb Mt. Marcy in the Adirondacks. I won a place every year and became an Eagle Scout with a bronze and gold "palm" as a result of my efforts.

Do the two approaches to life seem contradictory? They didn't seem so to me.

I also won a council scholarship to a five-week Scout "Wilderness Camp" in the Adirondacks. When I arrived I was known as the scholarship kid (at least I thought so), and realized that while my parents were unemployed (this was during the Great Depression), my companions were relatively "rich kids," the sons of professional people for the most part. I felt as if I didn't "fit in" because they talked about attending prep schools and what colleges they would attend and how one kid's father was a judge and another owned a hotel, etc. My parents had at the most six years of schooling and I thought I'd be lucky to get through high school.

During our first long canoe trip I avoided any real work around our campsites and believed I was being successful in doing so. One evening Mr. Dyke, a camp counselor and college student on summer break, approached me privately and said: "Gordon, in this camp we try to do as much as we can, rather than as little as possible." That was all. But with those words I realized why I was feeling so uncomfortable around the other kids. It was because they were involved and I wasn't. I began to volunteer—and did it badly until I got the hang of noticing what needed to be done and just doing it.

The greatest lesson I learned that summer was that if I pitched in and did the work that needed to be done, it took no more time or energy than avoiding it. For the first time I experienced the joy of harmoniously working with others for our mutual benefit and being accepted by the group. That experience changed my life and how I saw myself and others. It took me a few years to appreciate that Mr. Dyke was one of my formative mentors.

Yet what had he done, what had he not done, and how long did it take? First, he didn't criticize me. I was very experienced and skilled in the art of rejecting criticism—I had been doing it for my whole life. Second, he simply explained the culture of the camp and let me absorb and use that knowledge, and third, what he said took ten to twenty seconds—that's all.

He and I never had another serious conversation that summer and I never encountered him again—yet his image persists and his words linger in my mind and guide my behavior even fifty years later. The success of mentoring is as dependent on how the mentee responds, as well as on what the mentor does and how he or she does it.

A Mentee's Responsibilities

To hold up their end of the mentoring partnership, a proactive mentee will:
- Recognize that each partner will often make different investments in different amounts, and that mutual gain (of varying types) is the goal.
- Appreciate the mentor's help without holding him or her in awe, so no sense of inferiority, fear, or awkwardness invades the relationship.
- Welcome the mentor's interest and concerns.
- Learn and practice self-empowering behaviors.
- Be open to feedback—accept information the mentor provides without interpreting it as evaluation.

- Set realistic expectations with your mentor.
- Be open and sincere about your needs and deficiencies.
- Communicate problems clearly.
- Search for ways to achieve your objectives.
- Initiate reasonably frequent contact with your mentor.
- Follow through on commitments and seek help when necessary.
- Level with your mentor about feelings that are important to you.
- Contribute ideas for solving a given problem.
- Be willing to discuss failures as well as successes with your partner.
- Do anything possible and appropriate to build a solid relationship.
- Recognize that mutual respect, trust, and openness is the foundation for achieving mutual commitment to mutual goals.

As organizations increasingly adopt work teams as an operational given, our ability to use our differences as organizational assets become more critical. In our society, we have long extolled (but not always practiced) tolerance of people who are different from ourselves. The more tolerant we become, the easier it is to live together and interact cooperatively. But tolerance brings us only to ground zero. We accept, but tolerance does not cause us to seek. Tolerance is an essential first step in working with people who are different. With growing diversity in the workforce, it is time to actively seek out, invite, and bond with others who are quite different from ourselves *because they are different.*

The act of bringing out differences, searching for the special attributes of others and using these strengths in daily operations requires an investment of time and effort. The payoff for doing so can be great. Seeking out such diversity pays immediate and long-term dividends in employee productivity, team problem-solving, and product innovation, as well as an abundance of other rewards.

Creativity training tell us that innovative responses to challenges in the workplace flow largely from the associations made between the problem at hand and the knowledge, ideas, and experiences held or generated from within ourselves. If you want a variety of methods for attacking a problem, recruit participants with diverse backgrounds who can contribute a variety of components for a solution.

In mentee training, participants are sometimes engaged in an asset recognition exercise. Each person fills out a mentee skill matrix that reveals their individual skills, knowledge, and experiences. The participants also brainstorm to create a list of unusual occurrences, positive or negative, that they have experienced. (The Myers–Briggs Personality Preference Indicator can also be used to contribute to this pool of group knowledge.) Participants record their thoughts about their special attributes in a journal. Toward the end of the training, group members let each other know the results they feel comfortable in sharing.

Topics of discussion can cover everything from previous work assignments, games they played as children, hobbies, and special interests, to personal goals. Getting in touch with their uniqueness is structured to be safe, fun, and exciting. Exercises are designed to overcome the "there's nothing special about me" syndrome.

From this review process, group members develop a list of special contributions they can make when an opportunity arises or becomes visible to them. The net result is a better sense of their personal complexity and the group's diversity, a fuller appreciation of their individual experiences, and an enhanced self-image. But most important, group participants have a heightened awareness of what each individual can contribute to their work groups and the organization. Each person's primary assets are then explored in a positive context.

In one case, a secretary said, "I sing in the church choir." When the team explored this activity, they discovered that singing helped her in her breathing, voice control, vocal resonance, clarity of diction, and dramatic effect. All this became apparent as the team discussed this single-experience asset. With the help of several mentors, within a year she was regularly making formal sales presentations to groups of clients and customers, a totally new activity for her.

Casting out stereotypes begins when individuals project the special sides of their lives and thoughts. Then we can no longer view them as we have in the past. This is also true of ourselves. Important to this process is the group agreement of "no discounting" of any person, their experiences or ideas. This pledge of respect for the individual encourages the participants to reveal most, but certainly not all, of the special aspects of themselves. The group agrees in advance that anything revealed will be respected and treated with trust and confidence. Participants are also warned against gathering data on others for purposes of gossip or later negative use.

The benefits of these exercises include a greater sense of appreciation of oneself, greater understanding and use of each team member's abilities and potential, and greater applied synergy throughout the organization. It becomes clear that each person is a unique and precious resource, able to contribute to everyone's benefit.

Such exercises are of great value as each person learns more about themselves, and also better appreciates the special qualities of each person in the group. This type of exercise can help mentees construct a self-development agenda for a long time to come.

Mentee Effectiveness: Mentors Help—Mentees Do!

Traditionally, mentors have spent much of their time identifying needs that their mentees may not have realized were important, and guiding the mentee toward recognizing and closing those gaps. In the newest forms of mentoring, mentors are increasingly focusing on offering information about options and paths, and mentees play a larger role in deciding upon their goals and developing strategies for achieving them. For example, a mentee may derive help from his or her mentor in planning, organizing, and managing a career-development or self-development program—and he or she may also use the opportunity to learn how to receive and use others' help effectively.

Other techniques mentees want to learn include how to shape or describe problems for mentor consideration, select role models, develop a network of mentors, resolve any relationship problems that may develop with their mentor, and use problem-solving approaches. The also want to learn how to benefit from all three types of mentoring relationships (formal, informal, and situational), focus on the future rather than on failures and problems of the past, and select, interview, and attract a variety of mentors, to meet various personal needs.

Echoing to the Third Generation

The ancient Greeks believed that what we do for good or ill affects our descendants for three generations. Mentoring can have a very long "bottom line" beneficial effect, but its impact can span generations.

Shakespeare wrote "The evil that men do lives after them, the good is oft interred with their bones." Not so with mentoring. Of course, if the effects are evil, it isn't mentoring (by definition). The benefits of mentoring not only help the mentee throughout their life, but helps produce such a different person that they can create a healthier, more productive, and successful environment for their children, and they for their children. This has happened in my own life and the bottom line is still stretching into the future. Perhaps it is in yours as well.

Many of the life-shaping and life-broadening mentoring experiences and relationships I've had enabled me to help my children and they their children to better face an evolving world.

Education is one such area. Though both my parents

showed signs of being very bright, each had only very little formal education. I graduated from high school and expected to wind up working in a factory for all my working life, and if I was lucky, rising to first line supervisor.

However, while in military service, I encountered a series of mentors who through their behavior, conversation, and decision making demonstrated the essence of what a well educated and highly trained mind could do. This involved the abundance of ideas, flexibility of mind, a grasp of history and human development, and much more that went far beyond what they needed to do their specific job.

When I came out of service I was ready for college and did very well at it. But the influence of those early mentors still affects my life and the way I live it. My greatest satisfaction today is that their influence enabled me to help guide my children on the benefits of a good education and they built the platform on which their children are advancing today. What more do we want from mentoring?

Throughout human history effective mentoring has been very important in helping families rise to a better life than their parents were able to achieve. This is an especially important factor for community volunteers who mentor poor, disadvantaged, or troubled children. For each success, it can not only enhance their mentee's life, but enable them to better raise their children.

In the end, well-mentored mentees who gain significantly from the experience tend to become mentors—and highly effective ones at that.

CHAPTER SIX:
WORKING TOGETHER

A great deal of the mentoring that goes on in any organization occurs without any systematic plan. One person sees a need in another and simply aligns with the other person and if the would-be mentee agrees or is receptive to it, a relationship is formed. Yet much spontaneous mentoring occurs for such a short time that it may be over before either party recognizes it has occurred.

Similarly, a supervisor or group leader will find an occasion when mentoring would be helpful and simply does it. The recipient recognizes that the assistance has been helpful and moves to internalize it and use the learning.

Informal mentoring can last longer. The relationship grows from another connection, like when a teacher chooses to mentor a promising student in her or his specialty, or a supervisor chooses to groom an individual whose special abilities match a particular organizational need.

For example, Laurie started in a major retail chain as a charge-back operator handling and disposing of damaged or unsold goods from her store. It soon became obvious that she organized this new job so effectively that she was getting exceptional ratings by management teams of assessors.

She was then asked to train new personnel doing the same work at other stores. She performed so well on those assignments that she was encouraged by her store manager to increase the visits. Soon she was groomed to serve on the assessment team itself and help personnel in other stores better organize their work to improve their ratings during inspections. It worked!

Though she had more than one short-term mentor providing assistance, more is likely to occur.

CREATING A PRODUCTIVE MATCH

The issue of "interpersonal chemistry" is an important factor when matching mentors and mentees in formal mentoring programs. Some organizations hold "mixers" for potential mentors and mentees in the hope that "natural" pairings will form. Others use personality profile indicators (the Myers–Briggs type indicator is most common) to provide prospective partners with insight into their own and their potential counterpart's personality. But certain assumptions can be built into the decision to address the issue of interpersonal chemistry that may not be helpful in more current types of mentoring efforts.

The success of any on-the job mentoring relationship depends on what the mentor gives, whether the mentee is able to use what is offered, and how well the application of the information works. How does compatibility affect these three factors? Consider this comment from a military officer:

I spent three years in hell working for Commander X. He is a first-class SOB and I do mean first class. He's a tyrant, picky as hell, and he never lets up, but he's also a teacher—a great teacher. I learned—no, mastered—more from him about some very important things than I've learned in the rest of my career. I often think that he could have given me the same things without all of that nastiness, but that is the way he came—warts and all. Now that I survived, and there were times when I didn't think I would, I appreciate the mentoring he gave me.

This "stern taskmaster" model of mentoring is at the other end of the relationship spectrum from the amicable, compatible mentor we might like to have. But what drives the mentoring relationship-compatibility or gain, or something in between?

In formal programs that focus on advancing the career of the mentee and providing him or her with special opportunities and exposure, mentees are often in awe of their mentors, and fear "doing something stupid" in front of them. Understandably, such mentees may regard "empathy" and "friendly chemistry" as the key ingredients in a successful relationship. Yet in other cases where mentees are more self-confident and less affected by the rank and prestige of their mentor, compatibility is less important than the amount of valuable information the mentee can derive from the relationship.

If the organizational goal of a mentoring program is to benefit from the strengths of a diverse workforce, build exceptionally creative teams, or change the culture of the organization, mentees might do better working with mentors who have quite different personalities or backgrounds from themselves. There are many historical and literary mentoring relationships developed out of clashes between two quite different people who only gradually came to appreciate the strengths and virtues of each other as they worked together on some mutual problem or project. After all, synergy often results from a diversity of viewpoints. We tend to learn much more from people who think differently from us and even have a different culture or set of values.

Basic Conditions for a Partnership

Since a mentoring relationship goes beyond obligation and contains a degree of voluntary activity on both sides, organizations would do well to make sure the experience is rich and rewarding for both parties. Make sure that the participants set ground rules and develop shared expectations at the outset of the relationship.

In a formal mentoring program, both parties are invited to write down their expectations of the relationship in private, so they can freely think through their own needs and desires without being unduly influenced by their prospective partner. Even then, candor may be difficult, especially for the mentee, whose tendency to hedge in the beginning-before the relationship begins to produce trust-should not be too surprising. Consider the organization that encourages mentoring as part of a workforce-diversity program "to create a level playing field for all employees." A particular mentor and mentee may have quite different ideas of what they need to do (and can do) to ensure that the mentee can compete equitably. It is imperative that both define their expectations.

In many marriages, partners often levy expectations on each other without making them clear-cut. These often come to the fore when separation or divorce is in the offing or has occurred. Each partner or ex-partner may engage in the "blame game" where each feels betrayed by the other because they didn't conform to some expectation or set of expectations that was never made explicit until then.

These non-explicit expectations are often so ingrained in the upbringing of the couple that they are not aware of them. They may deal with their personal view of what a man or woman (their mate) should be like, the role they should assume, or the rules they should live by. When these assumptions are violated, there is often hell to pay.

In mentoring, if the mentee assumes the mentor will promote their career, and the mentor has been socialized in an organization that focuses on each person being responsible for their own careers, the gap can lead to disappointment and rancor unless these differences are brought out early in the relationship.

Organizational cultures can be as opaque to an outsider as family cultures. This is why getting to know all about the relationship is so critical. Each person needs to be very explicit about his or her own assumptions and expectations.

Drawing Up a Partnership Agreement

After sharing and resolving differences in perspective, expectations, and goals, it is time for each party to develop a set of specific, initial objectives or plans for the relationship. In an employer-sponsored program, these plans are often developed in cooperation with (or reviewed by) the mentoring coordinator. This person assists inexperienced mentors and mentees in developing workable plans and ensures that the organization's voice is heard.

When the initial plans or objectives have been developed, the coordinator often asks questions such as: Do you have any questions of me? What type of help or support do you want from me? What do you need to make the mentoring process go forward?

In this kind of formal mentoring program, it is not uncommon for the mentee to create a personal message for the mentor. They ask for specific types of help, and for the mentor to create a similar message for the mentee at the same time. For example, the mentee may write a statement such as:

I have set the following personal development plans that I want to achieve in the next six months ...

I need to know more about ...

I want to strengthen the following skills ...

I think you need to know this about me ... (In this case, a discussion may be preferable to a written statement.)

Alternatively, the mentee may ask a question such as: What would be most helpful for me to know about this organization or its culture? What changes or developments do you see in the organization's future? What behaviors are rewarded or discouraged in this environment? These questions indicate that the mentee is new to the organization, division, or location. They will help the mentee get a hold on things that are important but often not discussed—possibly to the mentee's regret.

On the other hand, the mentor may develop questions such as: What are the most important things you would like to get from this relationship? Here is a list of things I believe I am particularly good at—are any of them of particular interest to you? What developmental needs, knowledge, skills, insights, etc. would be of greatest value to you? What is your preferred method of learning: listening, visual images, hands-on, or observing? What can I do to increase the comfort level between us? What can each of us do to make sure we start off on the right track? Is there anything I need to know, (such as your likes, dislikes, or ways of doing things) that would be helpful to me? Is there anything I can do to increase your comfort level with me? What else is important to you?

Often such a partnership agreement is no more than a plan for what they both are aiming for and how they intend to go about getting there.

Logistics

It's often helpful for mentors and mentees in a formal mentoring program to draw up an agreement specifying a number of points, such as how, when, and where the partners will meet and work together. It is not unusual for organizations to set certain guidelines, such as, "Meetings during working hours will not exceed four hours a month."

Some of the common concerns that partners may have include:
- How often will we meet?
- How long will our meetings last?
- Where will we meet?
- Who will be responsible for setting up our meetings?
- When we meet: during lunch, before work, after work, or during work?
- How do we go about canceling a scheduled meeting if

necessary?
- What is the best way we can contact each other?
- What ideas do we have for getting our activities organized?
- How do we alter this agreement if it becomes necessary?

AN AGREEMENT—NOT A CONTRACT

Both parties need to understand that mentoring is a voluntary activity, and that the relationship is a no-fault one. Either partner can end it for any reason, or no reason. A mentor or a mentee can say, "I am ending our relationship," without having to justify the decision, and without being subjected to recriminations. If the mentor-mentee agreement were in any way enforceable, the interaction would involve obligation and cease to be mentoring, since the spirit of volunteerism would be gone.

This type of no-fault understanding is difficult for some individuals to accept. People often levy unwarranted expectations on others, which leads them to demand an explanation or feel hurt when a relationship ends. The partner may resort to phony justifications or even counter-recriminations in response. For this reason, an up-front understanding that no justifications will be given will help the parties adjust to any changes down the road.

Those who want to "hold someone to" the agreement are perhaps not ready for mentoring. They may be happier with a tutor, who would be more amenable to an enforceable contract.

The power of mentoring derives from its spirit of generosity, its altruism. In this way, mentoring is akin to a generalized love of others (which is often a prime motivator for mentoring). It can't be forced. However, because mentoring is inherently altruistic and focuses on benefiting the mentee, very few agreements are not carried out or modified without mutual agreement.

TOWARD A PRODUCTIVE RELATIONSHLP

For the mentor-mentee relationship to be productive, both parties might agree to some of the following:

- There is a punishment-free environment (mistakes are expected as part of the growth process).
- The goals must be mutual.
- The relationship must be based on a sense of mutual comfort and equality.
- The mentee takes risks and shows initiative.
- The mentor's role is to help and support.
- People who are significantly different from one another may be matched, so as to increase the potential for learn ing and skills development.
- Mentoring inherently involves personal change and growth, and as such friendship may grow from the association.

Each mentor/mentee relationship is unique, because each person is unique and each partner should recognize such differences.

Chapter Seven:
Training and Development

*M*entoring should not be hurried. Since the benefits of good mentoring can pay dividends for decades or a lifetime, the participant's training should not be compromised. Excellent mentor/mentee training is essential.

Mentoring as an Evolving Art

When we look back on the twentieth century, we tend to focus on the technological advances. These advances enabled humans to fly, have instant communication with other people around the world, and enjoy a fantastic variety of experiences, plays, music, news, and information in their own homes that no monarch could have commanded in 1890.

But technology only permits—people choose! Airplanes can be used to drop bombs as well as to visit relatives or reach an exotic vacation spot. The World Wide Web can be used as vehicle to bring higher education to your home, or fill your days and nights with trivia. Today most people can choose to build the life they want, to an unprecedented extent.

What we may fail to realize are the parallel advances we have made in the more human sciences. These can transform our inner lives in tremendous and meaningful ways.

In the United States, we no longer consider high school to be the completion of education and now embrace the need for lifelong learning. Creating a more democratic and inclusive society and upgrading the spread of social and communications skills and practices—of which mentoring is one example—is harder to measure, but is no less of a powerful phenomenon in today's societies.

The new technology enables us to expand the reach of our mentoring far beyond the face-to-face or snail mail limits of the early twentieth century. We can mentor a fellow passenger on a cross-country airplane trip, if the opportunity and need becomes apparent. We can also study the techniques of mentoring and communicate with other helping agents on our computers at home if we choose. And we can take training courses to master the emerging social skills we need to help build a more civil society.

Today we are more focused on building leadership skills in our organizations rather than just relying on past supervisory and management practices. Few organizations rely on training a new employee who serves customers to only run a cash register and an item scanner. The quality of the communications between co-workers and others has become an increasing key determinant of organizational success.

Like every other aspect of human cooperation, interpersonal trust and communication must flow freely in the twenty-first century organization. Mentor and mentee skills need to be updated, expanded, and renewed. They need to be more artful, subtle, and sophisticated as the complexity of the problems to be solved grow and becomes more challenging, but also more rewarding.

As the success of an organization becomes more dependent on the quality of interpersonal skills, mentoring calls for extensive training.

Achieving Mentor Competence and Confidence

The following table presents a typical set of mentor training modules for a two- or (preferably) three-day mentor training program (the difference often determines the level of skill achieved). While mentoring has been practiced for generations without any training (except possibly by emulation or personal invention), the stakes for organizations are too high to let employee development happen by chance. Since mentor training is designed to prepare participants to achieve unusually valuable results in a nontraditional training environment, course graduates should be able to demonstrate (not just understand) the essence of the mentoring experience and the knowledge and skills needed before they finish their training.

Just as a newly created supervisor or team leader would hardly be expected to operate in today's organizational environment without some interpersonal skills training, job or task definition, or procedural knowledge, we should not assume that people will operate effectively as mentors without similar training.

There are some crossover skills. For instance, today's supervisors are often trained in such arts as active listening and reflective feedback skills, interpersonal creative problem-solving techniques, and what disempowering behaviors to avoid. We need to recognize that when supervisors or leaders are expected to mentor their associates they may (or may not) have had such skills training depending on the organization that employs them.

Typical Mentor Training Modules

Lesson plans, audio/visual content, dynamic examples, and exercises to reinforce skills should be created or purchased for each module the trainer uses.

- What mentoring is and is not in an Information Age context.
- Mentor and mentee roles, relationships, and responsibilities.
- Have you been mentored? A self-awareness exercise.
- What mentors do and how they do it: skill building.
- What makes mentoring different and special. An awareness exercise.
- Designing an empowering mentor-mentee partnership.
- How to make the most of a given opportunity (situational mentoring).
- Key mentoring skills (including skills practice).
- Developing your own mentoring style.
- Understanding mentee needs.
- Reading mentee problem signals: cues and clues.
- Specific ways to help a person grow and develop.
- Positive behaviors to practice.
- Disempowering behaviors to avoid.
- Developing an appropriate mentor-mentee agreement,
- Examples of how to handle special cases and situations:
  Cross gender-cross culture and special uses of mentoring (as appropriate).
  Hierarchical considerations-new developments in organizational structures, i.e., delayered or team-based, etc.
- Using the Socratic method of development.
- Interpersonal creative problem solving techniques
- Enhancing one's teaching, coaching, and counseling skills.
- Active listening and reflective feedback: tools for better understanding of mentees and mentee empowerment—skill-building workshops.
- Experiencing the joys and achievements of mentoring.

If one has of these types of specific training, it may be enough for the trainer to connect that experience to their new roles of mentors as an expansion of their other roles. However, that doesn't seem to occur very often.

As new techniques are developed that can expand mentor or mentee performance, they should be added to their training just as would be done with supervisors or leaders.

MENTEE TRAINING: MAKING THE MOST OF BEING MENTORED

Until the last decade or two, mentee training was scarce to non-existent in most organizations. Mentees were believed to be passive recipients of the good things their mentors were doing for them. Even today, many organizations with some type of mentoring programs pay little attention to mentee skill development. This neglect can diminish the returns from mentoring activities.

Some organizations give lip service to mentee training by teaching potential mentees a little of what they will be mentored in. For example, an organization offering mentoring to participants in an "upward mobility" program provides training in what the program is about and the gains participants may accrue. Seldom do they concentrate on the enhancement of mentee skills and knowledge–on how to ensure that the mentoring relationship pays off.

Other organizations provide a day or two of training for mentees so they become active partners in the process and take some responsibility for their own development. The following table displays some typical mentee training modules.

Typical Mentee Training Modules

Lesson plans, audio/visual content, dynamic examples, and exercises to reinforce skills should be created or purchased for each module the trainer uses.

- The mentee's role and responsibilities as a proactive participant in the process.

- How to recognize, seize, and retain the core lesson in each mentoring transaction.
- How to distill the essence of a mentoring experience.
- Practice in listening skills as they apply to being mentored.
- How to interact most effectively with a helping agent.
- How to plan, organize, and manage a self-development program based on assistance from a mentor or mentors.
- How to select, interview, and attract a mentor or mentors.
- How to develop a tentative mentoring agreement that incorporates the elements the mentee considers important.
- How to use the "discovery method" of self-development. (Creating a set of exploratory task options for a mentees to pursue.)
- How to use and work with multiple mentors: variations on networking with a purpose.
- Identifying, analyzing and confronting negative transactions.
- How to glean ideas and essential information from situational mentoring exercises.
- How to seek, assess, and use appropriate role models.
- Developing and maintaining an adult-to-adult relation ship in the partnership.
- Keeping the relationship balanced (giving back to one's mentor).

Good mentor and mentee training leads to greater adaptive behavior in each partner and a more productive and satisfying relationship in the long run. Training in proactive mentee skills offers an organization paybacks of enormous potential in an age where the need for life-long learning and idea exchange is increasing.

Skills training can help a mentee recognize, internalize, process, and apply their mentor's help much more effectively than they are able to do without such training. A degree of combined mentor/mentee training can also improve the performance of each partner. Effective training methods include:

Participant sharing and analysis of their past experiences with mentoring. Such discussion can lead participants to recognize the imaginative component of high-performance mentoring, and better understand how these results are achieved by connecting themselves with their own experiences and those of others in the training group.

Dramatic true stories presented in an audiovisual format. Stories of mentors who achieve exceptional results have a considerable impact on trainees when they have the opportunity to analyze what the mentors did and how they did it.

"Improvs" and other theatrical techniques. These weaken existing "role constraints," or inhibitions that sometimes interfere with the easy and comfortable flow of ideas and information between mentor and mentee.

Demonstrations and role-playing exercises. These help participants practice listening and feedback techniques, which can contribute to mentee empowerment and aid in their problem-solving. One group of participants act as mentees, and share their own aspirations in a consultative environment, with other class members acting as mentors. Then the roles are reversed.

Case studies. These help participants share viewpoints and ideas on ways to help prospective mentees.

Training for mentoring partners can often make the difference between a so-so or failed program and one of great success and ongoing long-term payoffs.

USING "COMMUNITIES OF PRACTICE"

Some organizations extend and vary training experience of their mentors through a technique called Communities of Practice (C of P). This approach to group learning and practice recognizes that people frequently help each other solidify their Knowledge,

Skills, and Abilities (KSAs) from training programs, introduce new and more varied know-how from outside the field of mentoring to the group, and update the mentoring knowledge base as the practice evolves.

A community of practice in mentoring involves creating a group of mentors (and possibly mentees) that meet periodically (often monthly after their formal training) for updating and strengthening their common skills, as well as tackling new mentee needs and sharing what techniques work better. In a way it is a training group, but when problems are brought into the open and uncommon ways to solve them are explored, it also becomes a support group.

I remember one situation that occurred in a church-based C of P group. A young man was trying to mentor a teenager in his neighborhood who had been in trouble with the police. Several times a week he would invite the teen to shoot hoops with him at a local recreation center. During a meeting with the group, the man said they seemed to get along well together and this formerly tense and angry young man was becoming much more relaxed.

At the next meeting, the young man reported that the teenager had gotten in trouble with the police again and he felt like a failure as a mentor. A small group of mentors on the spot pointed out that many factors impinge on any person and not all mentees can solve all of their problems, even with the help of an excellent mentor. The young man had not necessarily failed—he had no way to assess what the teen had internalized to benefit him later in life, if not at present.

One of the mentors walked the young man through the steps to become a "mentor advocate" for his mentee during the mentee's juvenile court appearance and accompanied his new mentor/mentee to court, to be with the youth when he had his session in court. The youth was paroled to his mentor and has not had a repeat offense for the last year and a half.

The teenager said he was "amazed" that so many people

had been interested in helping him, and now volunteers to help younger students with their reading at a local church-based after school program. The youth's whole demeanor changed, though at times his temper flares. He and his mentor are working on that problem.

This local Community of Mentoring Practice has lasted for eight years and is still operating.

CHAPTER EIGHT:
SPECIAL MENTORING ISSUES

Some organizations and individuals experience "cultural lag" regarding mentoring and the kinds of cultures that best support it. Many are stuck in the dying hierarchical model of organizations that are "top down." Yet, when those old barriers to more democratic forms of mentoring come down, fresh needs and opportunities are discovered and these organizations often embrace newer beliefs and processes.

Other issues may also arise. The competitive forces in the marketplace can highlight the costs versus the gains derived from mentoring. As mentors refine the ways in which they help others, they may bring new interpersonal concerns to the forefront-nuances of the art of mentoring.

Today most of the problems associated with mentoring fall into at least seven categories.

1. Refocusing attention from career advancement to personal development.
2. The social costs of a formal system, i.e., How much control should be relinquished or added?
3. The "Fagin Factor"–the problem of negative counsel.
4. Compensation and incentives.
5. Certification, credentials, diplomas, and licenses.
6. Litigation-free mentoring.
7. Gender, sex, and harassment concerns.

To achieve the gains that mentoring promises, we need to take a fresh look at such issues. Doing so may challenge some of our assumptions about career advancement and the helping relationship itself.

REFOCUSING ATTENTION TO PERSONAL EMPLOYEE DEVELOPMENT

A few decades ago, our cultural norms operated on the assumption that everyone in business was interested primarily in getting ahead, advancing in their job field or climbing the organizational ladder. At that time, promotions were either the sole prerogatives of management or controlled by contract or custom, as with seniority. Mentoring was often seen as solely a device for preparing people to improve their personal situation. Unfortunately, many other employees were not seen as able to benefit from mentoring.

In today's organization, the view that mentoring is only a way of getting ahead may be unrealistic. Yet the "getting ahead" ethic is so pervasive that other aspects of mentoring–such as creating a balanced, more able person–may get lost in the shuffle. Some employees see mentoring only in terms of its relationship to internal programs such as upward mobility or cross-training (and the rewards associated with them), or as a way of gaining credits before a selection panel. Some individuals are shocked and disappointed to discover that their mentors are not sponsoring them for a specific type of job advancement.

Part of the culture shift from a focus on advancement up the career ladder to self-development has come about through the practice of "downsizing" and "delayering" in many of the later and more successful organizations.

As personal computers, information systems, and organization-wide common data bases became more widespread, it became clear that many data handlers and other support personnel were no longer needed. Layoffs of thousands, and in some larger organizations tens of thousands of people, have occurred.

This "downsizing" was most often accompanied by "delayering" of the tall pyramidal organizational structure. The primary function of many mid-level managers had largely been the task gathering data from subordinate organizations "massaging" it (which often subtly altered its meaning), and passing it up the ladder where other managers combined it with that of other units and passed it up one more step. The data was largely late and "fudged" to make sure nothing negative in a manager's subordinate organizational units would be seen by the eyes of those above. Delayering of these no-longer-needed middle manager jobs reduced the potential and opportunities for career ladder-type advancement.

While there is nothing wrong with wanting to advance in one's trade or profession, a person's well-being has other dimensions—such as personal happiness, job satisfaction, and the joys of achievement in another field. However, the fact that there are games other than "King of the Hill," will not have much appeal for those who never see the other parts of the playground.

Mentoring holds a far more sophisticated promise. Until quite recently, upper management and the professions in business and government were filled with people who had devoted much of their lives to the art of advancing their careers. This ability to advance defined success. All the things that mentoring is good at bringing forth—adaptability, creativity, imagination, a sense of balance, vision, insight, the utility of our feelings, intuition, caring for others, a sense of sharing and helping—were largely ignored. Yet these are the capacities that today's successful, proactive leaders need in abundance.

Until a thirst for self-development comes in balance with the hunger for getting ahead, we are unlikely to nurture the organizational leaders needed for the future.

THE SOCIAL COSTS OF A FORMAL SYSTEM: HOW MUCH CONTROL?

A leading proponent of the measurement and control school of management has been quoted as saying, "If it can't be measured, it hasn't happened!"

But how do you measure internal change in a person—the blending of everything learned and every skill mastered—to bring about a subtle shift in a person's leadership style? How do you measure the consequences of listening to a senior sales representative talk about the subtlety of a customer service transaction, then internalizing that subtlety as part of your behavior when dealing with other customers? How can you really measure a life-changing experience, the fruits of which a person uses again and again throughout their life to help others achieve their goals?

Even if it was possible to measure the ten of thousands of such transactions each day, would that make the measurement cost effective? Part of mentoring is an art form, dependent on the imagination of the participants. While the organization may have legitimate goals for a formal mentoring system, too great an effort to control the process can produce a paint-by-the-numbers piece of art.

Those who believe that most individuals are incapable of creativity, spontaneous synergism, and artful personal development will probably continue to treat mentoring as a simple input/output device.

Some companies have designed mentoring programs so that participants understand why the organization chose mentoring as a device for exceptional personal development and what the employer expects as a result. These programs convey the idea that management trusts people to get the job done. In these operations, costs are minimal and mentees arrange to get what they need without significant burden on the system.

As more organizations seek to create a healthy and productive workplace and self-directed, empowered personnel, they adopt mentoring as a support for their evolving and adaptive culture. These organizations recognize mentoring as a pervasive instrument for bonding employees in a network of flexible caring and sharing relationships. They envision evolution of the helping organization where information and ideas flow easily to the points of greatest utility, making the organization (and its components) proactive, efficient, productive, and competitive. This is in stark contrast to cultures that still encourage the hoarding of knowledge, compartmentalization of activities, and bureaucratic control, where suspicion and animosity thrive.

THE "FAGIN FACTOR"—THE PROBLEM OF NEGATIVE COUNSEL

In his book *Oliver Twist*, Charles Dickens portrays Fagin as a criminal beyond redemption. However, Fagin did take in a number of homeless boys. He fed them, provided a place to stay, and taught survival skills (thievery). Clearly, Fagin was serving his own interests, but at least he was helping boys who had few prospects for survival in the slums of nineteenth century London.

The Fagin character may seem long ago. I have, however, heard and observed business executives-people who fancied themselves to be mentors-offering advice to less sophisticated individuals on price fixing, questionable tax avoidance techniques, falsifying official records, lying to investigative agencies, bribery, and a multitude of other high crimes and misdemeanors. These suggestions were handed out with confident admonitions of "No one will ever know" or "Everyone does it"—generalizations that sometimes will lead to a jail cell.

Most people understand the positive focus of mentoring. But when it comes to encouraging employees to mentor, they may come to recognize a hard truth: Some people make poor mentors. As one corporate vice president put it, "We have people around here I wouldn't want to mentor a warthog. Their advice is terrible. They are out of touch and out of date."

There is no easy answer to the problem of "inappropriate mentors." Some organizations screen mentors and invite those with poor mentoring skills to take on administrative roles, or become advocates for the program. The best answer seems to be better training. This includes both experiential training in which peers influence each other, as well as class exercises in analyzing interpersonal transactions that help prospective mentors correct inappropriate attitudes and behaviors.

COMPENSATION AND INCENTIVES

It has been argued that you can't hire a mentor. Once a mentor invests in receiving a tangible pay-out, the spirit of mentoring departs. The freely given help of a mentor is compromised, and the organization (or even the mentee) has leverage to extract something.

One professional society has a very popular "rent a mentor" program underway which has failed to grasp the essence of the relationship. The members of that society, many of whom are frustrated because they do not have the background they need to practice successfully in their chosen field, recognized that a highly experienced person in their discipline could provide insightful, incisive help in specific areas. The program hopes to attract technical experts who can also focus on members' welfare and development. They could just hire a consultant tutor or coach rather than a mentor, and call a spade a spade, but they hope for more.

Similar problems arise when an organization "requires" someone to serve as a mentor, makes mentoring subject to evaluation or performance appraisal, or provides extra compensation to the mentor for taking on that responsibility. Organizations that tried this approach have found they needed burdensome and expensive measurements to "ensure" that the mentors were doing their jobs. Others found that they tended to attract mentors who were more focused on the extra income than on the help they could give—the personnel who applied for the position of mentor most vigorously were the least likely to be effective mentors. If financial compensation of any form accrues to the mentor, the selection should be very carefully done, if at all. However, since most rules may have exceptions, we offer one example in the box on the following page, "Mentoring in Real Estate Sales," where mentor and mentee split a fee.

MENTORING IN REAL ESTATE SALES

Mentoring in real estate sales is different than mentoring in most other organizations. The primary difference is that neither the mentor nor the mentee are paid a salary. One of the primary assets of a real estate salesperson is time. Time focused on any activity other than working directly with a buyer or a seller must somehow produce prospects or revenue. Consequently, mentors are usually compensated by receiving a share of the commissions earned by the mentee.

Mentoring in real estate is not designed to provide promotional opportunities to higher positions for two reasons: 1. There is only a three or four step hierarchy in even a large real estate company—agent to sales manager to vice president/division director to president (usually owner). 2. Many successful agents have higher incomes than their managers.

Some real estate agents question the advisability of becoming a mentor. Some do it because they like to be of assistance to other people. Others have learned to structure mentoring in a way that increases their income enough to make it worthwhile. Mentoring also creates the opportunity to get onerous tasks done by someone else for a period of time. In addition, there is a good possibility that the mentor can learn from the mentee. The skills and behavior in listing and selling real estate are so varied that mentors can learn from mentees who have different backgrounds and skills than they do.

For the mentee, mentoring provides an opportunity to get a head start on much of the explicit and tacit learning necessary to be a successful real estate agent. While the 60 hour training course required to get a license and the up-front training offered by most companies provide the ABCs of the business, observing the activities and having the guidance of an experienced agent supplements the mentee's knowledge and skills. It makes possible the internalization of subtle clues, untold rules of thumb, underlying assumptions, and implicit relationships with clients, customers, and service providers in the industry. This often makes the difference between the successful and the highly successful new agent.

Some of the areas of mentoring relate to the big picture of sales and listings, followed by the many details in each of those activities. Another important area of learning is the computer technology designed specifically for real estate, some of it mandatory, some of it essential for top producers. Mentees can also benefit from the less tangible, but extremely important sales skills which include listening, problem solving with buyers and sellers, negotiating, and conflict resolution.

One major method of mentoring is "Follow me around" or shadowing. The mentee is expected to attend sales meetings, go on listing appointments, attend settlements, and tag along to meetings with buyers which includes showing houses. Since the mentee is expected to generate prospects, the mentor will at times be the one to tag along and assist as needed until the mentee is comfortable carrying out the duties and responsibilities required.

The mentor should provide the mentee with the reading materials generated in past transactions including, but not limited to, copies of listing agreements and contracts with all the required documentation. Other reading materials include company manuals, financing information provided by lenders, and magazines from the many real estate associations including the National Association of Realtors.

The final result of a worthwhile mentoring experience can be a new agent on the way to being a successful real estate agent, or a new member of the mentor's team (perhaps the first member), or a new long- or short-term partner.

For the mentor it can mean new insights and sharper skills in working with people, plus the rewarding feeling of having been a part of the growth of another person.

David Booker, realtor
Long & Foster Real Estate, Inc. 150 Elden Street, Herndon, VA 20170
David@davidbooker.com

CETIFICATION, CREDENTIALS, DIPLOMAS, AND LICENSES

As the advanced societies in the last two centuries became more technologically complex, education levels rose to absorb and transfer the exponentially exploding knowledge and skills being brought on line from the physical and human sciences. As more people pursued personal learning, the realms of the "experts" grew. But how do you ensure that presumed experts really understand and can practice the knowledge, skills, and abilities they profess to have mastered?

In a rapidly growing number of fields of knowledge, certification, credentials, diplomas, and licences have ballooned and the need for certainty of competence becomes ever more critical.

Whole new realms of proof have emerged with computers, information systems, security concerns, and a host of other critical realms—and the increase in attention to such issues is not likely to lessen.

The search for certainty of competence has created new areas for mentoring because of the subtlety of the art, the special quality of the relationship and the ability to impart information quickly on a one-to-one basis. The use of mentors in professional certification has seen an especially sharp rise.

LITIGATION-FREE MENTORING

Some organizations are still stuck on mentoring as a career advancement tool rather than as a human development tool. It is not surprising that these "protégés" play the Industrial Age games of comparing the power, prestige, and position of their mentors with those "assigned" to others and believe that they have come up short. This "disparate mentoring," as they see it, has led to a few lawsuits and even to some courts (where the old notions of mentoring hold sway) taking the charges seriously.

DISPARATE MENTORING

In 1993, the US District Court for Maryland ruled that a female psychiatrist could pursue a claim of "disparate mentoring" under Title VII of the Civil Rights Act. In the psychiatrist's suit, she alleged that compared with her male peers, she received less mentoring and that her mentor had less influence and prestige than the mentors of the other people in a fellowship program at the National Institutes for Mental Health in Bethesda, Maryland. She also claimed that the difference in mentoring was motivated by "sexual animus."

The court rejected a recommendation to dismiss the suit and ruled that mentoring could be considered a "term, condition, and privilege of employment," similar to job assignments and training opportunities. The use of the term "protegé" was cited as implying a special emphasis on preparing these employees for special treatment and that the relative power of the mentors was a possible factor in "disparate treatment."

"Unfortunately," said the director of the Mentor Foundation, "the judge was apparently reacting to the way mentoring was practiced in that organization. Some changes in philosophy, goals, practices, and training would have created a mentoring system so fair as to be virtually immune to successful legal action."

When the mentoring relationship is a partnership of equals, the mentee often sets the agenda and initiates the connection. The mentee makes things happen, and the relationship is voluntary on both sides. Either party can terminate for any reason or no reason. With such a system in place, there is no basis for a lawsuit unless either party (or both) is involved in something that has nothing to do with mentoring.

GENDER, SEX, AND HARASSMENT CONCERNS

Workplace romance has been around as long as there has been a workplace. Sexual issues in the workplace have become more complex, and with sexual harassment legislation, less common and less focused on the extraction of favors in either direction.

A decade or so ago, the media gave sensational coverage to a few cases of sexual favoritism that were tied directly to mentoring as the lure or at least the incipient incident. However, all of those cases were based on relationships where career climbing, favoritism, and extraordinary treatment were part of the scenario. If the same events happened in the new mentoring environment, they would be treated as grievances by co-workers or handled under equal employment opportunity laws.

Nevertheless, we do need to look at this issue. The caring, sharing, and helping essential to an effective mentoring relationship does tend to produce a closeness, affection, and even love (sex is another issue) between the partners. No one should be surprised if this produces warm feelings. However, affection need not lead to more base relationships in mentoring any more than in other close working relationships. It should also be recognized that this sense of closeness is often what provides the enthusiasm and synergistic benefits from the mentoring relationship. The feelings that develop can be either a boon or the source of a serious blunder, depending on how the participants handle these feelings.

As our society, our workforce, and our organizational cultures continue to evolve in sophistication, interpersonal competence and general sensitivity to more nuanced facets of our personal abilities and uniqueness, new issues will arise that can benefit from mentoring. Some of the aforementioned concerns are already in decline in frequency of occurrence (such as gender, sex, and harassment issues) because of the attention and training given in recent years. Yet they can still be of importance in some organizations and special situations. Perhaps our greatest challenge is to detect and deal effectively with such new problems and opportunities.

Chapter Nine:
Examples of Current
Mentoring Applications

*A*lmost daily new applications of mentoring are encountered, suggesting that the potential is limited only by our imagination. This chapter surveys the growing variety of applications, both inside and peripheral to organizations. These uses of mentoring are not exotic. All have solid, productive track records frequently in more than one organization or the environment and society in which they operate. The skill with which they are practiced largely determines the value they produce.

Volunteer Mentoring in our Communities

One of the most powerful and important mentoring activities for employing organizations is the voluntary work occurring with youth—especially at-risk or disadvantaged young people performed by their employees.

From stay-in-school programs to literacy efforts, from math tutoring in after school church programs to an added social dimension to sports activities at local community centers, these programs help young people through some of their toughest years.

Often you are likely to hear calls on your local media for volunteer mentors to help needful youth. These include formal programs such as America's Promise, Big Brother, and Big Sister, and short-term help in reading enhancement programs in local grade schools as well as Girl Scout or Boy Scout merit badge counselors who share their expertise (and may offer even more).

It is impossible to tell how many people are involved in such mentoring efforts, because so many programs are informal and no reporting system is in place. However, I've heard estimates of three to five million mentors in the U.S. alone; over the years those people probably work with three times that number of mentees. And many people consider these estimates to be quite low.

Nearly every time I stop at a restaurant for coffee after teaching an evening class or out shopping in a mall having a crafts show, I see groups of young people in tow of several adults who are their mentors. The same is true of visiting an art gallery or museum or watching a teenage sporting event on the weekend. These events are often run by adults intent on building youth success, and cumulatively a better and more effective society for our future.

Often these mentors are engaged (though often unaware, or not focused on the implications of their work) in also building a more effective workforce for the future.

BUSINESS-TO-BUSINESS MENTORING

The U.S. Department of Defense (DOD) has set aside funds for some defense contractors to mentor their subcontractors and suppliers. The DOD recognized the importance of having broad-based reliable sources of supply, and it wanted the suppliers to be stable companies staffed with competent personnel and competitive within their industries. Through mentoring, the department encouraged its contractors to help their vendors meet defense specifications, operate efficiently, and enter new markets.

Nationally, mentoring is being handled by organizations such as SCORE (Senior Corps of Retired Executives), an organization that matches retired executive volunteers with novice entrepreneurs to help them with their specific needs and get them on their way to creating a successful venture.

SCORE mentoring does not stop once the business takes off. Many entrepreneurs are able to create businesses, but succumb to obstacles that prevent these enterprises from becoming the enduring ventures their owners are working so hard to secure. A mentor's expertise can often provide the entrepreneur with the perspective needed to overcome those obstacles.

In the area of business-to-business relationships in manufacturing, it is becoming more common for manufacturers to mentor their customers' personnel. For decades, some companies have provided training for their users to ensure effective handling, maintenance, and repair of their products. But as product complexity increases, training alone may no longer be enough. Software programs in particular are often underused because so much of their value comes from applying a program's more sophisticated features to new challenges in the user's work. In this instance, a mentor can help the user explore her or his special options—many of which are not identifiable until after the user has mastered the intended applications.

Transition Mentoring

When faced with the prospects of large-scale reductions in force, some organizations use internal and external mentors to help employees face the challenge of the transition. This voluntary support—which goes beyond the employer's outplacement services—not only helps the individuals who leave, but also has a positive effect on the survivors. They see their organization as a more caring and helpful place.

In a similar situation, terminated employees who subsequently find new employment form support groups for those who have been recently laid off. Those veterans of downsizing are able to share skills and knowledge that point others to new careers or reemployment.

Because it is now much more common for individuals to make multiple job and career changes within their lifetimes, mentors can also assist people in reexamining their aspirations, goals, and levels of satisfaction from time to time. This assistance can lead to a new career within the organization, with a new employer, or even into an entrepreneurial venture. Once frowned upon by management, these career shifts often create an invigorated, enthusiastic employee who brings refreshing ideas, new perspectives, and innovative approaches to the job. Mentors also can help their associates approach their work with a fresh or different perspective.

MENTOR OR MENTEE, OR BOTH?

Under the heading "Power Connection," Frank Swobodo and Warren Brown in a *Washington Post* article (April 3, 1994) related how CEOs of some of America's largest corporations had been beating a path to the door of Jack Welch, chief executive officer of General Electric Corporation.

Titans in their own right, the heads of such firms as General Motors, International Business Machines Corporation, and Eastman-Kodak Company had gone to the undisputed champion of corporate reorganization. In the 13 years since taking over GE, Welch had cut its workforce in half, positioned the company so that every line of their business is first or second in its industry, and raised its revenue from $26 billion to more than $60 billion.

Swoboda and Brown refered to the meetings as the "CEOs Club," and said this type of contact makes a larger point about managing. "In today's increasingly competitive climate, traditionally inbred corporations are being forced to look outside to keep up with the best business practices." Many CEO contacts were by phone, and it was not uncommon for Welch to invite them over to share ideas. Welch constantly preached the need for executives to get outside their own organizations to see what works best and then to borrow those techniques or ideas. Welch spent much time personally visiting other companies. Consequently, Welch's attitude made it easier for other executives to seek him out. This is Information Age networking at its most productive.

But, of greater significance here is that these meetings and telephone calls represented a series of classic mentoring sessions, with Welch as mentor and the other CEOs—for the moment—as mentees. Of course, no one called it mentoring. Memories of proteges, sponsorships, and older and wiser relationships still hang heavy in the air.

Update and Peer Mentoring

Since the above article was published (retained to demonstrate how much mentoring today varies from the Industrial Age model) Jack Welch has retired, but still works with six CEOs of major corporations. From Welch's recently published biography, *Straight From the Gut* and his statements on television interviews, these associates interact as peers and the leadership in any given meeting (often on the golf course) may vary depending on who has the best idea, the most knowledge, or the freshest technique. Thus a lot of cross-mentoring goes on spontaneously.

MENTORING IN THE FAMILY AND COMMUNITY

There have always been individuals scattered through all societies who invested personal time energy and knowledge in helping others achieve more than they would have without such help. When a retiree says, "I raised my children—I'm mentoring my grandchildren," he is making an important statement. He is saying that he provided his children with their physical and survival needs, but allowed the schools and other social institutions to round out their development. He now recognizes there are many aspects of character development—values, social behavior, creativity, compassion—that should not be entrusted to strangers. As some grandparents are raising grandkids, more recognize they must also invest in their "development."

More people are seeing a need to contribute their special learning and talent in helping young people in their communities. This is accomplished most often through churches, schools and civic associations. These volunteers seize specific opportunities to help a young person gain a new vision of life's potential, and help them to succeed despite life's obstacles. This type of helpful intervention is becoming more common and systematic, and also contributes to creating a more civil and successful society.

For example: Montgomery County, Maryland hosts a task force on mentoring based on the belief that mentoring makes a big constructive difference in community life. Their goals include promoting mentor program awareness; connecting mentoring programs; providing information about mentoring to program sponsors, the general public, and potential participants; promoting the public's involvement in mentoring; and assisting communities within the county in organizing mentoring programs.

Specific efforts include bringing mentoring organizations together through organizing and maintaining local mentor and mentoring networks, publishing a Montgomery County mentor program directory, providing information and technical assistance to mentoring programs, and providing information and referrals and sponsoring annual mentor conferences.

The most dynamic results are being achieved in the County's mentoring program for children and youth. The essence of this activity is captured on the next page.

Montgomery County, Maryland Task Force Goals for Children and Youth

- Supporting school and home interaction
- Encouraging high academic achievement
- Graduating from high school
- Making plans for future schooling and employment
- Promoting positive peer relationships
- Promoting parental involvement in children's education at home
- Promoting parental school involvement
- Encouraging student participation in school Honors programs
- Training high school students to be mentors of younger students and others

WITHIN THE ORGANIZATION

Much of the recent growth in mentoring has come through the proliferation of mentoring activities sponsored or managed by an organization to advance the agendas of specific individuals or groups, or to meet intensified organizational needs. Examples include:

Entry-Level Personnel. In the past, a few of the larger, more stable organizations welcomed the arrival of special groups of new management or technical college graduates (mostly scientists or engineers) as interns entitled to a period of mentoring. In recent times, companies are adding groups of apprentices and skilled technicians—as well as experienced personnel and even managers who are entering a new corporate culture—to the ranks of their formal mentoring programs.

Career Enhancement Programs. As organizations move from steeply sloped pyramids and ladder structures to the downsized and delayered pancake model, they become more aware of the career needs of virtually all employees. The career-building programs of today, many of which warrant the help of a mentor, tend to be more systematic and modeled on a mentor/mentee partnership-such as when Individual Development Plans (IDPs) are used to chart a person's career advancement.

Breaking through the Glass Ceiling. Today's proliferation of women's programs provides an excellent example of special purpose mentoring. These programs aim at achieving a more balanced technical and managerial workforce.

Workforce Diversity. These programs are designed to create a level playing field for members of racial and ethnic minorities. By enabling diverse individuals to participate and contribute more equally to the advancement of the organization, more people benefit. Diversity programs respond to the fact that the workforce is becoming more varied and that mentoring is one way to ensure we move from an exclusive hierarchy to a more open and equitable organization.

Team Building. As a company changes from a highly individualistic and competitive work environment to a more cooperative team culture, employees may find that they don't know how to be truly cooperative and trusting. While training in teamwork and group problem-solving processes help a great deal, many organizations are also developing mentors to help team members (and some managers) get over their competitive "hang-ups," which interfere with group synergy.

Total Quality Management (TQM) Efforts. TQM is a sound concept and critical to America's competitiveness here and abroad. However, the emphasis on control of people and machines, as well as the need to measure everything with statistics, can become so burdensome as to stifle originality. In some cases, the obsession with proving results (alleged gains) has raised costs and imperiled the program. As an antidote, some organizations empower mentors to work with individuals and teams alike to streamline their efforts, reduce costs, and rekindle enthusiasm. TQM enthusiasts, experts, and advocates are often cast in the mentoring role.

Conserving Organizational Memory and Know-How. Many organizations realize the consequences of losing skilled and knowledgeable people through precipitous downsizing and early retirement. It is becoming increasingly common for these organizations to ask departing employees to cross-train and mentor the people who will remain, before the mentor exits.

Rebuilding Organizational Trust. Downsizing erodes the basis for employee trust. Well-trained mentors are a viable link in rebuilding and maintaining this important element of organizational culture. Even though the trust that develops is often interpersonal rather than institutional, surviving employees tend to feel less alienated, more involved, and in some ways more secure when they have a mentor to help them address their concerns and problems. The sincere helpfulness of an effective mentor can help recreate an environment of trust.

Accelerated Transfer of Technical Skills and Knowledge. In today's fast-paced environment—where "speed is life," as Tom Peters is fond of saying—people need to fill the cracks in their knowledge and skills as rapidly as possible. A technical mentoring network not only enhances their efforts to master their field but also strengthens their ability to adapt to rapidly evolving technology and change. Transfer of technical know- how is one of the oldest forms of mentoring, and growing more complex and critical each day.

Leadership Development. Some leaders have always used mentoring to enhance the competence and performance of those they lead. Great leaders tend to do this with exceptional skill and grace. But we are now moving away from the notion of leader as an all-knowing commander to the recognition that organizational success is built on the cumulative effect of tens of thousands of less majestic decisions. A myriad of mentors operating throughout the organization can improve the quality and beneficial effect of those decisions.

Effective leaders regard personal mentoring—and encouraging those who are mentored to expand the circle—as one of their greatest opportunities to invest in building a successful organization. The list of innovative uses of mentoring presented here is far from complete. As a basic component of one-on-one employee development, the variety of applications is almost certain to grow in number and quality.

APPENDICES

INTRODUCTION

A rapidly increasing number of private firms, nonprofit organizations, governmental agencies (at all levels), associations, and academic institutions are creating or operating formal mentoring programs.

This segment of *The Mentoring Organization* focuses on helping mentoring advocates in such organizations design, develop, and implement a new program (pilot), or update or strengthen an existing one.

App. Figure 1 (page 118), "Mentoring Systems Diagram–Pilot Program" is the distillation of the experiences of more than thirty large and small organizations over a ten-year period. Since then it has been used, (with some variations based on different objectives and the populations from which they drew their mentors and mentees), by over three hundred organizations.

These appendices offer a step-by-step approach (33 of them) to planning, developing, operating, and successfully concluding everything from a first effort to a formal mentoring program. Some organizations have used this system to plan revisions or improvements to their existing programs. Others have used it to discover gaps and errors in their original design that led to disappointing results, or even to the dropping of a previous program.

Each step offers appropriate commentary, suggestions, and questions that need to be asked, and procedural information for

Mentoring Systems Diagram ~ Pilot Program

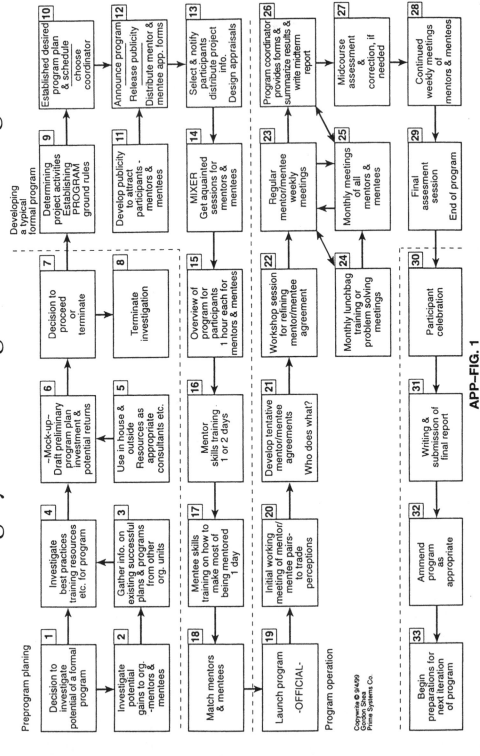

APP–FIG. 1

that step or stage. Also included are sample forms, suggested activities, and resources that might be helpful to your team in advancing their work.

However, it is important to realize that this material is intended as a source for ideas, a study of the best practices and useful aids. The design of a formal mentoring program cannot be done effectively through a "one size fits all" procedure. Your program must meet your objectives, serve your organization and its participants, and evolve to meet new challenges and opportunities.

We hope that this material will speed you on your way to operating an ongoing, highly productive mentoring program. We also suggest that you revisit page 46 "Characteristics of Different Types of Mentoring." This figure is used to illustrate how a successful formal mentoring program can produce a variety of beneficial results among the mentor and mentee populations. This diagram is a more detailed version of the chart on page 41, "Spectrum of Mentoring Interactions." It illustrates how the training mentors and mentees receive in a formal program feeds back into ongoing informal and situational mentoring activities with other people in the organization and off the job.

APPENDIX ONE:

PREPROGRAM PLANNING

*U*ntil the 1980s, most formal mentoring programs concentrated on advancing the careers of select groups of people such as management interns, or increased the sharing of information and techniques between technical and/or professional personnel. The model was top-down, senior to novice.

As organizations shift to the more "downsized" and "delayered" flatter structures, mentoring has become a more democratic instrument for developing the knowledge, skills, and abilities (KSAs) of virtually every employee. In today's more farsighted organizations, mentoring offers more opportunities for supporting cultures of increasing inclusion, flexibility, and geographic dispersion.

As we move through the steps for planning the type of program that will best suit your organizational needs, there are three fundamental questions that should be asked. These relate to the anticipated future of the organization overall, and the people within it, now and in the foreseeable future. These are:
- What are the Outcome Objectives for your overall program?
- What outcomes do you envision for your mentors?
- What outcomes would best serve the needs of your mentees?

Outcome Objectives are quite different from the way people usually set objectives. Most people will list a variety of objectives for any general goal, and often confuse process objectives with outcomes.

A process objective identifies the step needed to achieve a goal, such as "train all mentors in the tools and techniques of mentoring." An Outcome Objective describes the conditions that prevail when the program is achieving its results. For instance: "A network of mentors and mentees are interacting productively and comfortably on a regular, as needed, basis across the whole organization."

In the first instance, you have identified a process step—a readiness to act—where in the second, an ongoing process has actually happened and produced results.

The results you seek can be limited or expansive depending on the resources and mandate you receive to set up a mentoring program. It can also be informal, and spontaneous, or very formally structured. In any case, envision what the organization and its people would be like if successful. This helps to focus the design appropriately.

Although the appendices deal with a pilot program, results should be envisioned in a broader and deeper context.

For the Organization

1. Is our organization moving away from a "command and control" culture toward one of greater self-managed, flexible, team operations?
2. Will our personnel be able to practice their mentoring skills effectively in a rapidly evolving technological environment to keep us ahead of general developments?
3. Will this program improve our recruitment and retention rates?

Answers to such questions are needed to describe the program in outcome terms.

What of the Mentors?

- Will they be experienced enough to use their skills, within their families or as community volunteers, to improve the general social environment in which their jobs exist?
- Will they recognize their ability to help other employees extends beyond the limits of their job description or professional competence?
- Will they recognize situations where they may need to be mentored and be willing to approach others to serve as temporary mentors to them?

What of the Mentees?

- Will they recognize situations where they need to seek help
- Will they possess the Knowledge, Skills, and Abilities needed to serve as a mentor when another person comes to them for assistance? (This may seem to be a stretch, but it happens).
- Will they be sufficiently sensitive and alert to grasp the essence of their mentor's help, to make it their own and change themselves as needed?

If you can answer such questions through your program design, you are likely to have a winning program!

STEP 1: INVESTIGATE THE POTENTIAL
OF A FORMAL MENTORING PROGRAM

You may have already decided to create, enhance, or revitalize a formal mentoring program. If you have the organizational power to accomplish this and need no help, you may consider Step 1 accomplished and move on. However, there is much to be gained from a close examination of this first step. In can be used to uncover other problems or opportunities that can be derived from a more broad-based approach.

Teams of like-minded people develop the most successful and long-lasting formal programs. They work together in the design and implementation phases as a task force or a committee of volunteers. When I use the term "you," I mean all those involved in such an effort. Consequently, your first task is to recruit other people to help you.

The next task is to decide and make explicit what you hope to achieve from the program, such as why you are interested in establishing a formal mentoring program. What needs will it meet and what opportunities will be gained?

When you and/or your investigating team initiate the program, or are researching the possibility of creating such a program, seven fundamental questions need to be answered.

1. What is the impetus for such a program? What is the rationale for the effort? What are its desired objectives, goals, or outcomes?
2. Who are the sponsors and what do *they* hope to gain or accomplish through such a program?
3. What authority are you operating under or relying on? (Note: This can be moral, legal, budgetary, or related to long-term employee needs, such as recruiting and retention. You may want to revisit the list of potential gains

for the organization, mentors, and potential mentees in the introductory chapter of this book.)

4. Where do you envision such a program would be implemented: company-wide, one department, or anything in between?

5. When do you perceive the mentoring activity for each pair would start and how long would it last; or would it be ongoing indefinitely with many iterations?

6. How do you envision such a program will be designed, developed, and implemented, recognizing that this topic is being discussed very early in the game and nothing need be firm at this point?

7. Why would your organization be willing to sponsor, help, and invest in such a program?

Remember, at this point you are only exploring the potential of such a program. Many conclusions, firm assumptions, and details will make for inflexibility before you know what the final program will be like. Keep an open and flexible mind for unforeseen opportunities for gains. If you are the sole owner of the idea, you may want to ponder these questions yourself or use them as items for group discussion if others are advocates and already working with you. Keep a record or have someone write down the essential initial responses to these questions.

When you consider the initial purposes, concerns, or problems to solve, you may find that such issues are more widespread in the organization than previously considered. Following is a checklist of common needs that organizations meet through formal mentoring programs. Check the items that you and your team believe may complement, supplement, or embody your own objectives.

Mentoring can serve:
- as a powerful recruiting tool
- as an effective new employee induction and orientation tool
- to assist employees in their career planning
- to help people new to the workplace succeed on the job
- to help employees cross-train each other
- to increase employee and cultural diversity
- to enhance retention of current and future employees
- to strengthen employee leadership skills at all levels
- to enhance or manage succession planning efforts
- to build intra team skills
- to encourage the sharing of technical information and skills
- to preserve and spread organizational memory, technology and culture
- Other* _____
- Other* _____
- Other* _____

*Add your own items to supplement those checked above.

Discuss the items you consider particularly important with your team in order to gain perspective on the decision making. Individuals often get enthused about the prospects to serve as volunteers for part or all of the program's development.

Do you have a mandate or charter for such a program? Does your authority to launch a mentoring program come with the position you hold and fall within your jurisdiction? If not, how can you or your team acquire such sponsors?

If you are a staff specialist, are you working on someone else's authority, or must you solicit support from a line manager? What if you want to encourage people in other areas to get with your program or start one of their own? Do you need to sell your program to others? Do you need to connect your concept to other organizational needs or initiatives such as diversity, recruitment, or leadership development?

Naive people often clamor for "top management support" for their program and complain when they can't even get top management attention. If you design a solid program with enduring benefits to your organization and its people, mentoring will not be another management fad that blossoms and fades. Many fine mentoring programs have resulted from the missionary zeal of a group who believe in its value, rather than from the edicts of top management.

From where and whom can you draw the expertise, approval, and assistance you need?

1. Expertise _____

_____

_____

2. Approval _____

_____

_____

3. Assistance _____

_____

_____

If at this point you and/or your team need further study, move on to Step 2.

STEP 2: INVESTIGATE POTENTIAL GAINS TO YOUR ORGANIZATION AND YOUR MENTORS AND MENTEES

The best way to convince yourself of the value of a mentoring program is to list the benefits to those involved in developing or sponsoring and promoting the program.

If you develop, operate, and improve over time a successful mentoring program (or several), benefits will accrue to your organization and its mentors and mentees often far beyond those mentioned elsewhere in this book. It is important for your development team to develop your own list.

General Gains for the Organization

- Formal programs often include significant training for mentors and mentees, creating a growing cadre of trained and experienced personnel. They will carry with them and use their mentoring Knowledge, Skills, and Abilities (KSAs) wherever they go in your organization, and for as long as they remain.
- People who serve as learning links within an organization refer their mentees to specialists, subject matter experts, and other special helpers when the expertise that is needed is beyond their own knowledge. This creates bonds that bring company personnel closer together and broadens the mentee's perspective of the organization's people resources.
- The relationship usually builds employee trust in the organization and a measure of loyalty because of the expressed investment in the employee. This lowers resistance to change and opens greater acceptance to evolving cultural shifts and new organizational models such as "Self-Managed Teams" and "Communities of Practice."

Example of General Developmental Gains for Mentors

- The acquisition of powerful and special leadership skills that are seldom available from any other source.
- Feedback from mentees keep mentors in the loop of what is really going on at lower levels or distant parts of the organization
- Mentors who gain a broad perspective of mentoring are more inclined to seek out mentors' assistance themselves, and hence become more able.

Example of General Benefits Available to Mentees

- The evolution from mentee to mentor is a common consequence of being mentored in a formal and well-structured mentoring relationship. Mentees gain first-hand experience in dealing with what mentors do and how to do it.
- Proactive mentees who benefit from a formal mentoring relationship set their own career and developmental plans more solidly and seek out and recruit appropriate mentors to carry them out.
- The primary reason to measure the results of being mentored can be deceptive. *Each mentee will internalize learning differently, link it to their unique life-learning reservoir, and use the learning over a long period of time to solve a variety of problems.* The only results that can really be measured accurately are short-term, very specific, and all too often superficial objectives.

Again depending on the design, the inclusiveness, and the type, and quality of training the mentors and mentees receive, gains to the organization, and the partners in the relationship can range from modest and brief to enormous and decades long.

Mentoring is much more than a program for your organization and the participants. Mentoring is a relationship that takes a person beyond their job requirements, duties, or obligations. It becomes an attitude, a skill set, and a commitment to helping others to become all that they can be.

Even a short-term personal failure can be turned by a mentee into a long-term success. A principle and insight shared by a mentor can be remembered and carried forward, and used by a more seasoned and mature person to solve a current problem, make a better decision, or provide a critical input to a team solution. A mentee's learning preserves valuable organizational memory, and becomes part of the intellectual and motivational capital of your organization.

Much of what passes between mentor and mentee is informal, or highly personal learning, as are the lessons drawn from it. Mentoring complements other training and educational efforts, often in critical ways. These unique lessons can provide a competitive edge, a starting point for generating creative ideas, and the source of fresh thinking in a group environment.

Quality mentoring also can produce beneficial external spin-offs in the employee's family, neighborhood, and community. Since effective mentors share their knowledge, skills, and experience with others they meet and deal with, it has often been said that "mentors are helping to build a more civil society."

STEP 3: GATHER INFORMATION ON EXISTING PLANS AND PROGRAMS

The more diverse and geographically scattered an organization is, the more likely that parts of the organization have existing mentoring programs, tried and failed to establish a viable program, or are seeking to establish a program.

Finding out what your organization is doing or plans to do in the realm of mentoring can save you time and effort, and avoid potential competition and the mistakes of others.

Before broadcasting your intent and asking for help, ideas,

and interest, have a clear statement of purpose. Define the populations you want to serve, relationships to be achieved, the stage you are at now, and how they might respond to you. It should be clear that you and your team are talking about a formal program.

To search for other mentoring programs in your organization, inquire about related programs your organization is involved with that cover at least part of your areas of interest, such as service activities in the community, mentoring programs sponsored by professional associations, and strategic partnerships with a mentoring component. Alignment with such groups may increase the organization's interest in your efforts.

If you broadcast your appeal on your organization's intranet, you may need clearances or reviews of your material. Telephone contacts with members of the Human Resources department can do part of the job.

Evaluating the responses you receive will probably require considerable thought and analysis. How closely does another program meet your needs or objectives? Will it be feasible to partner with another program? Will your efforts complement or conflict with other programs? What can you learn from them? What insights and practices can you share with others as your activity develops?

If you and your design team finds that an earlier program failed, or worked for a while and then went out of business, find out why. Ask questions such as: Was the length of the formal relationships too long or too short? Was that program too burdensome for the participants? Were their objectives too narrow for your type of organization? Was the program unable to inspire the participants?

The failures of a small percentage of mentoring programs were most often caused by not attracting enough mentors or mentees. When we have been asked to rescue such a failing program, we have found that the reason was a lack of genuine mentoring and the fun and achievement that real mentoring offers.

When analyzing other mentoring programs in your organization or some of its other outreach programs, determine what makes them successful. Looking at the structure and content of any failed program may also be instructive.

Gathering Information on Existing Successful Plans and Programs

Look within your organization
- Survey other organizational units
- Survey personnel for ideas and experience
- Study the art of turning past failures into successes

Look outside of your organization
- Survey others in your business or profession
- Gather information and ideas from others in your field
- Research the Internet for similar start-up programs

Look at special purpose programs
- Choose the right questions to ask
- Distinguish differences in goals and objectives
- Build on the successes of others
- Conduct further research and readings

STEP 4: INVESTIGATE BEST PRACTICES AND RESOURCES FOR YOUR PROPOSED PROGRAM

What is available to help you design the most effective mentoring program for you, your associates, and your organization? A common approach is to search out so-called Best Practices.

But best practices for whom?

There is no standard formula to produce the ideal mentoring program. Design the best program you can for your organization, test it by running a pilot program, and then develop the model that will best serve your needs in the future. Some people are always in search of standard solutions that will guarantee quality results, but such thinking can be a trap.

You and your team will decide what practices will best suit your people's needs and offer the greatest opportunities. This is where your unfettered imagination should roam *before* you start making decisions about what is practical or desirable.

In any group, there is great wisdom if its members are open to diverse ideas and not wedded to single answer solutions, and do not feel their particular view must prevail.

If your design team sets consensus above interpersonal competition and contributes their best ideas, expect them to evolve over time as other ideas and knowledge is added to the mix. Do not get distracted by prevailing beliefs. This combination creates the potential for a truly great Mentoring program. A team dedicated to producing elegant solutions by simple methods is well positioned to produce highly workable and enduring program elements that will best suit the practical processes the mentoring partners need for best results.

Search the literature, interview other practitioners, and examine successful case studies (especially this book) to get ideas for your own design. These should be collected, examined, and sorted for use.

But a parallel process should also be explored and that is to set "Outcome Objectives" for your program. Remember an *outcome objective* is focused on describing exactly what you want your organization, the mentors and mentees and the goals you are working to achieve, to be like if your mentoring program is successful. The best practices you select should contribute directly to those results.

For example:
One hospital in a very labor tight area set this outcome objective for its "welfare to work" program:
"Hire the next 20 people sent to us on a random basis by

the welfare agency to fill that number of entry level jobs and achieve a six-month retention rate of at least 80 percent with that proportion of the new hires also being rated as "fully satisfactory" by their supervisors.

"Each such new hire will be assigned a mentor from their new department and the mentor and the supervisor will work together to ensure these objectives are met."

Sound simple? Well it wasn't, but the first four groups developed an *esprit de corps*, excellent relations with their mentors and supervisor and enthusiasm for their work. The outcome objectives were exceeded with every group, thereby relieving the shortage of entry level employees in several departments.

Working backwards to mentoring "best practices" this hospital's management relied heavily on in-depth training of their mentors and mentees in such areas as: active listening; reflective feedback techniques; team building; interpersonal problem solving methods; empathy awareness exercises; productive confrontation processes ("I" message development) and career guidance. After two years, 72 percent of the first four groups were still employed at the hospital, and 38 percent have had one or more job upgrades. Management considers this as an exceptional success rate compared to previously hired similar, non-mentored individuals.

RELATED GAINS

The decision to create, support, and maintain a mentoring system engenders many opportunities. There are spin-offs, a multitude of ways to lengthen and strengthen the beneficial effects, and constant opportunities to enhance the quality of transactions between mentors and mentees, often with little or no additional costs.

Unfortunately, creators of a mentoring program are so focused on their program's objectives they may miss opportunities for synergistic collaboration with potentially related programs, policies, and people. For example.

- Mentors who detect a problem in their mentee's work life that they feel inadequate to address, may be able to refer that person to an existing employee assistance program (EAP) or provide other help their mentee may not be aware of.
- Referrals to other mentors in the organizational network who have special expertise or strengths can be helpful to their mentees without disturbing their own partnering relationship.
- Synergy in acquiring other mentor's help and/or mentor skills for themselves can be obtained from related training and development programs such as leadership, stress management, or time management, as well as to help participants in those programs.

Write down some of the ways that this future mentoring program might interface with other activities in your organization to strengthen them or to draw strength from them: _____

_____

_____

_____

_____

_____

_____

_____

_____

_____

Step 5: Use In-House and Outside Resources as Appopriate

Some years ago, my associates and I developed a training and consulting program titled "How to Design, Implement, and Manage a Successful Mentoring Program." This three-day program consisted of a two-day seminar/workshop and a one-day of subsrquent follow-up consultation. The two day seminar/workshop prepared key staff members (largely the program's design team) to plan a cost-effective, state of the art mentoring program for their organization and adapt it to their own unique environment. At the end of the workshop, participants had in-hand their own plan for meeting the objectives that they set forth. After they met with other affected personnel and organizational units, the mentor/trainer served as a resource consultant to the design team.

To our surprise, we often found that the client's personnel had seldom explored the connections and experience of people currently within their own organization. These resources were often close to hand and when contacted, eager to help.

In Step 3 you investigated successful in-house organization mentoring programs-past, present, and even developing programs. Any such activities can provide useful inputs (including what to avoid) and ideas that you may want to graft onto your evolving program. Some people involved in those programs can augment your design team's efforts. However, your design team should remain lean, with a clear and sharp focus on your program's objectives and avoid scattering your efforts.

Outside consultants can offer perspective and ideas, ask penetrating questions, and identify lesser-known resources. The tendency of some groups to "go it alone" sometimes lead to inadequate design and even failure.

Step 6: Mock–Up Draft of Preliminary Program Plan

This step is the most complex, crucial, and potentially risky set of activities. Your plan must be solid enough to cover all reasonable contingencies and possess a good chance of meeting your objectives. You may want to discuss this step with a broad audience before proceeding.

Many development/design teams go through the flow chart one step at a time to discuss the implications, requirements, and gains at each item, thereby creating a mock-up as they go along.

For example: Sometimes, who will be mentors and mentees is not completely clear. If your program focuses on mentee career development who will be the mentees—new hires or those longest in grade? Do you need a mixer so that partners can self-select each other or will someone (and if so, who) make the matches for them? How much training should mentors receive? How much training and what kind for mentees? What will be the ground rules for the partners etc.?

At this point, these issues need not be resolved in detail, but the outlines should be sketched. The design team should resolve when there has been enough discussion on a given issue.

The same applies to the anticipated costs and benefits. Is it likely that a mentoring organization culture will evolve out of the program? How much of the intended mentor training can be classed as leadership, management, or communications training? How much more effective will the program be if mentees are well trained in the art of being mentored? How often and for how long should mentors and mentees meet with each other?

Discussing such topics and questions in an organized fashion more than once is well worth the effort for building a successful program.

Mentoring has a myriad of potential long term rewards. Like leadership training, mentor and mentee training builds developmental skills that can be used throughout that person's total work life to the continuous benefit of your organization. Like most human resources development efforts, this is not an accounting exercise. It is skill and knowledge building as an investment in its people and the organization's future. This is where vision comes in. A pro and con list of gains and time investment for the typical pair of partners can be developed to provide perspective on the effort.

As we move deeper into the information age, our people needed to manage and use our most critical and expandable resource, the creativity, enthusiasm, and commitment from within each person employed with our organization.

STEP 7: DECIDE TO PROCEED OR TERMINATE

Based on your or your investigative team's systematic analysis of the investment and effort needed to design, implement, and manage a formal mentoring program, and your assessment of the anticipated gains from doing so, you should be ready to proceed with, or terminate your work.

This decision need not be an irrevocable decision. Organizational factors may change, new leadership or management may emerge, the winds of financial fortune may shift, the tightness or looseness of the labor market can vary, and many other changes can favor resuscitation of a dropped program or cause a program in progress to be expanded or modified.

This is a logical point to stop for a moment and take stock of where you are, and ascertain if you want to move forward. By now you have more information and ideas than you did at Step 1.

You may choose to move forward, but perhaps in different

ways, for different reasons and with modified goals. This pause can provide breathing space for more mature reflection on your options. Often an hour-long meeting is enough for many groups, where others will want to get away from the problem for awhile and let things settle before making a decision.

Most groups choose to proceed, but feel they are doing so in a less pressured environment, and better able to apply perspective. They may also choose to set other "pause points" for assessment, consideration, and decisions on how to proceed before moving on.

If you decide to advance, are there other things you want to factor in? If not, proceed to Step 9, if not go to Step 8.

Step 8: Decision to Terminate
Mentoring Systems

If your organization decides not to proceed with establishing a formal in-house mentoring system at this time, you may want preserve the research findings you have accumulated about mentoring for any of three reasons.

1. The interest in mentoring may arise again for similar or quite different reasons. New organizational initiatives, evolving markets, or changes in the available workforce may provide renewed impetus for serious mentoring. An evolving desire to participate in community affairs, prepare more employees for overseas assignments, or a change in top management could precipitate the need for building a future mentoring program.

2. Even if a formal program is not justified at this time, you may want to provide voluntary "lunch bag" training sessions for those people who will mentor anyway, informally or in short bursts as situations arise in the workplace between associates. Some organizations gain the beneficial effects in employee assistance to each other at little or no cost or effort based on an employee's innate altruism and willingness to help each other grow and develop.

3. Organizational growth and success may rebalance the rationale for future mentoring in its favor.

List the current justifications for abandoning mentoring efforts so that they can be reevaluated as time goes on:

APPENDIX TWO:

DEVELOPING A FORMAL

MENTORING PROGRAM

*T*he steps offered in Appendix Two can produce a variety of effective mentoring programs. An important component for creating one that best serves your organization can be formed by the tweaking of these factors and processes, based on the research, sensitivity, and creativity of your design team.

The preparation phase of a pilot program is critical, whether you are creating your first "formal" program, revising an existing one, or expanding the use of mentoring more broadly throughout your organization.

There are four main activities to be carried out simultaneously throughout this phase:

- *Publicity*: Garner support, recruit participants, and educate employees at all levels of your organization on the nature of mentoring and the purpose of your program.
- *Recruitment*: Gather volunteer mentors and mentees, orient them on the goals and requirements of the program, and ensure that the partners are well in formed to carry out the program objectives.
- *Matching Mentors and Mentees*: Establish a system of pairing mentors and mentees for best results.
- *Training and Development*: Educate participants and the program's support personnel.

The project team also needs to make a host of decisions, design forms, and set the program ground rules. These include developing the program plan and schedule, choosing a coordinator, setting up a management plan, and designing appraisal forms. Sample forms are included in some of the steps in this part of the appendix.

The four activities listed above usually require a deeper look at the details than is often the case in launching a new or revised program such as mentoring. For instance:

Publicity goes far deeper than just promotion. People throughout your organization need to be re-educated as to what mentoring means in the 21st century. Explaining the utility of a neural-type network of mentors to adapt to Information Age organizational structures is also important. Mentor and mentee expectations need to be dealt with realistically.

Recruitment means attracting and involving the right types of people for the right reasons. Only your team, with consultation with potential participants, can decide which people are right. Mentoring can be used to meet diversity goals, build self-managed teams, and/or encourage lifelong learning throughout the organization. Each such organizational goal might suggest different individuals as participants. Where are the needs and/or opportunities greatest?

Matching Mentors and Mentees can be done in different ways. Some organizations hold a "mixer" or other informal meetings to allow the partners to get acquainted and make a match between themselves. Other programs use highly structured resumes and "needs surveys" to pair people. Each method has long range implications for the organization and its people.

Training and Development has three steps specifically designated for participants. These program "overviews" for mentors and mentees and the training courses for each is critical. How much time and content your organization provides for such activities reflects their investment in participant competence and performance. In programs ranging from a half-day to three days, the program benefits are directly related to the training time invested.

Participants and their sponsors should remember that mentoring when done well, has a "career-long bottom line" and keeps people fresh and involved.

Note: Gordon Shea's two companion books, titled *Mentoring—How to Develop Successful Mentor Behaviors* for mentors and *Making the Most of Being Mentored* for mentees, provide a variety of checklists, training exercises, and case studies for individual analysis or small group discussion. These workbooks provide a variety of training exercises, case studies for individual analysis and small group discussions, and checklists. Thought-provoking course content includes self-analysis sheets, challenging ideas, and insightful perspectives. Check out these resources when developing your training program.

STEP 9: DETERMINE PROJECT ACTIVITES AND ESTABLISH GROUND RULES

The mentoring design team needs to make tentative decisions about the details as to how the actual program will operate (Steps 19–31) and a first cut of the schedule of such events. Any unique features or variations from the systems model should be included (or deleted) and the final items arranged for easy tracking by all members of the team.

Beware of the tendency to weigh, measure, and *quantify* much about mentoring. The typical example of "reduce turnover by 12 percent" or "improve retention by 12 percent" is probably not a reasonable outcome to set for mentoring, or for mentors. Each mentee will decide for themselves whether they stay or go, based on many subjective factors that may have nothing to do with the company's best efforts—nor the mentor's. However, an effective mentor can have a great influence on the feelings of their mentees toward themselves, their mentor, and the overall organization.

By contrast, a set of basic assumptions or ground rules to be shared might well include such items as:

"There are no promises of career advancement, protection from adversity, or special treatment because of participation in this program. There is mutual effort toward mentee development and the personal rewards that such efforts bring to each partner."

- "No promises of career advancement" is aimed at disabusing mentees of the idea that the program is aimed at fast-tracking them to rapidly climb the career ladder.
- "Protection from adversity" means that if a layoff comes, they are treated as other employees, depending on company needs, and factors such as skill needs and relative longevity.
- "Special treatment" means it is up to each mentee to make as much of the experience as they can during and after the program is over.

Here are more ground rules. Choose what will be useful to you, or modify them to fit:

- The relationship is voluntary for each party.
- A mentor and their mentee should not be in the same "chain of command" (if one still exists in your organization).
- The mentor and mentee each need their supervisor's approval to participate.
- A mentor's guidance/counsel is not to supersede that of the mentee's supervisor's in matters that are the supervisor's responsibility.
- Mentors and mentees must attend the scheduled training.
- Mentor and mentee partners must develop and adhere to

their mentoring agreements unless exceptional circumstances dictate otherwise.

- Active involvement of both partners is necessary.
- Trust, confidentiality, and candor between mentoring partners must prevail at all times.
- All personal conduct must be consistent with the personal and professional standards set by your employer.
- Mentors and mentees each manages their own expectations and responsibilities with their partner.
- No fault/no reasons need be given to end the partnership.
- Mid-course and final evaluation survey forms must be filled out by each partner.
- Either partner can contact the mentoring coordinator for ongoing support as needed.

Such ground rules help each partner know where the boundaries are, and yet should not be burdensome nor impede the work to be done.

STEP 10: ESTABLISH DESIRED PROGRAM PLAN AND SCHEDULE—CHOOSING A MENTORING COORDINATOR

In this section are two examples of easy to understand project or program schedules. The design team may want to also establish a PERT/CPM project chart for their own planning purposes, but this is not an ideal way to communicate the schedule to other users.

The job description and duties of the mentoring coordinator may need to be expanded or curtailed to meet the needs of the job in your program or situation.

The question of how long a mentor and mentees should work together in a formal mentoring program arises at this point. A range of three months to one year tends to be most productive. This allows for about a dozen to some 50 weekly meetings (each of an hour or so). While the length of time depends on the goals set for the mentee, most organizations tend to run their pilot program for a six-month limit. When working on a pilot program, you can lengthen the project development time instead of arbitrarily picking a fixed amount of time the partners work together this early in the program development stage.

It is also fairly common for some of these relationships to continue on an informal basis when the participating pairs find that worthwhile. Some of these relationships also develop into friendships that can last for years.

In some organizations, mentors will be in short supply, which limits the length of the planned formal relationship.

Mentor Coordinator's Functions

The mentoring coordinator facilitates and encourages mentoring activities in designated units or divisions of the organization. The mentoring coordinator plays an important role in mustering support and interest in mentoring and in providing administrative assistance but is not involved in any aspect of individual mentoring activities between the mentors and their mentees.

The mentoring coordinator is supported by the mentoring management team, (and any consultants assigned to the team), which assists with all tasks including the planning of initial orientation meetings with senior management personnel. These are usually on-site briefings about the program and an introductory presentation to people interested in the mentoring program. The collaboration between the development team and the program coordinator continues throughout the duration of the mentoring term and often involve exchanges of messages, requests for information, and receipt of supportive material via E-mail. The mentoring coordinator can also help design and monitor pilot programs for different mentoring populations.

SPECIFIC TASKS AND ACTIVITIES

Activities for the mentoring coordinator are divided into three segments:

1. Program promotion and organization.
2. Continuous program assessment and communications support.
3. Conducting program assessments and developing reports.

Typical Program Promotion and Organization Activities
- Schedule initial meeting with a team of supporters or division's senior management.
- Schedule introductory presentation to persons interested in learning about mentoring even if they do not plan to participate in this pilot or its iterations.
- Schedule training sessions for mentors and mentees.
- Circulate promotional material about introductory presentation(s) and specify time and place.
- Identify and contract for appropriate site for the mentor training sessions.
- Identify and contract for appropriate site and facilities for the mentee training sessions.
- Attend meetings with senior management and mentoring teams related to this program and other activities as appropriate.
- Review with mentoring team operations of the program and scheduling of training.
- Participate in introductory presentations. Circulate self-assessment guides for mentors and mentees mid-term and at the end of each iteration. Collect those completed forms and instruct on how to forward those if necessary, and the need to be completed by a specific date.

- Review self -assessment guides and prepare lists of mentors and mentees.
- Advise selected mentors and mentees on their participation and the requirements for training and ensure that tasks have been completed in time.
- In collaboration with consultants, confirm one-to-one terms of agreement between mentors and mentees.

Continuous Program Assessment and Communications Support

- Implement E-mail link with consultants.
- If possible, oversee creating a mentoring website on the organization's intranet.
- Collect mentoring agreements.
- Collect periodic assessment forms.
- Forward inquires and comments to consultants or man aging teams.
- Forward material and communications from consultants to mentoring teams.

Program Assessment

- Collect final assessment forms from mentoring teams.
- Review assessments (possibly with consultants).
- Write or assist consultants or writers in preparing the final report.

MENTORING PROGRAM PLANNING AND SCHEDULING CHART

Phase	Date	Event
Phase I	Oct. 11	Initial Planning Meeting
	Oct. 24	1st Task Force Meeting
Phase II	Nov. 2	MBR Meeting & Briefing
	Nov. 6	1st Announcement
	Nov. 16	Mentee Briefing
	Nov. 30	Mentor Briefing
	Dec. 14	Mixer
	Dec. 18	Selection/Matching
Phase III	Jan. 9, 10	1/2 Day Training Sessions Mentees
	Jan. 23	2nd Day Training for Mentors
	Jan. 24	Launch
	Jan. 24	Monthly Program
	March	Monthly Program
	April	Monthly Program
	April 30	Halfway
	May	Monthly Program
	June	Monthly Program
Phase IV	July	Celebration
	July/Aug.	Evaluation
	Oct.	Begin New Program

MENTORING PROGRAM PROJECT MANAGEMENT SCHEDULE

	Nov	Dec	Jan	Feb	Mar	Apr	May	June	July	Aug	Sept.	Oct.	Nov.
Phase I Planning & Preparation	█												
Phase II Organizational Preparation		█											
Phase III Participant Team Formation		█											
Phase IV Participant Skills Training			█										
Phase V – Program Implementation & Support Workshop			█	█	█	█	█	█	█	█	█	█	█
Six Month Assessment									█				
Assessment— End of Cycle I Begin New Cycle													█

*Schedule assumes a Ten Month First Cycle operation of *Formal Mentoring Program* — cycle time could be adjusted after six month assessment or at end of first year to meet operating needs of the organization.

Step 11: Develop Publicity to Attarct Support and Recruit Participants

Because of the time needed to develop publicity materials, gain approvals, and reach potential participants and allow time for them to respond, the design team should begin to develop promotional, publicity, and recruitment material parallel to Step 9 and as soon as possible. Promotional materials may need to explain what mentoring means in a modern context and how it is used in this organization, because so many people hold outdated notions about mentoring.

A look at APP. Figure 1 (page 118), "Mentoring Systems Diagram–Pilot Program" identifies most parts of a step-by-step general promotional and publicity plan to carry your group through all the necessary phases of the program.

Details of your mentor and mentee training program may not be clear at the moment, but those that are should be listed so advanced planning, time, and resources can begin to be allocated for that activity.

The design team should include a person knowledgeable about the channels, media, and special informational outlets within (and possibly beyond) the organization. A person familiar with such things as each media's deadlines, editorial guidelines, and style of presentation can also be invaluable. If such expertise is not available, it might be possible to ask the design team for volunteers to develop such knowledge within the team. See the suggested Publicity Planning sheets below. The Design Team and possibly others should help in filling out these sheets.

PUBLICITY AUDIENCE PLANNING SHEET

What organizational units and participant groups will be effected by the mentoring program?

1. _____
2. _____
3. _____
4. _____
5. _____
6. _____
7. _____
8. _____
9. _____
10. _____
11. _____
12. _____
13. _____
14. _____
15. _____
16. _____
17. _____
18. _____
19. _____
20. _____

What individuals, organizational units, or resource persons should be notified of the plans for this mentoring program?

1. _____
2. _____
3. _____
4. _____
5. _____
6. _____
7. _____
8. _____
9. _____
10. _____
11. _____
12. _____
13. _____
14. _____
15. _____
16. _____
17. _____
18. _____
19. _____
20. _____

What individuals, organizational units, or resource people could provide useful feedback or contribute to this program, if they were notified early?

1. _____
2. _____
3. _____
4. _____
5. _____
6. _____
7. _____
8. _____
9. _____
10. _____
11. _____
12. _____
13. _____
14. _____
15. _____
16. _____
17. _____
18. _____
19. _____
20. _____

Step 12: Announce Program, Release Publicity, and Distribute Forms

Coinciding with announcement of the program, release the details of the program including its aims, benefits, and rationale to achieve maximum impact and support.

In this section are sample mentor and mentee application forms. Modify these forms to suit the needs and aims of your program. Divide your forms into front and back sections of a single sheet to allow respondents more space for writing their statement.

Pilot Mentoring Program Mentor Application Form

Name:_____ Work phone:_____

Job title: _____ Fax: _____

In company address:_____

E-mail: _____ Work location:_____

Best time/day to be reached:_____

For the information below, use the reverse side or attachment if more space is needed. Please reference item number if you are continuing.

1. Work, educational, and training background (Please include major areas of experience, expertise, etc.):_____

_____

2. Job experience (List job titles, place employed, and number of years). List only for the last five years: _____

_____

3. Identify special Knowledge, Skills, and Abilities (What I'm good at.): _____

_____

4. Discuss why you wish to be a mentor: _____

_____

5. Are you willing to meet regularly (at least two to four hours a month) with your mentee? (The mentor program committee recommends weekly meetings.)
   Yes _____ No _____ If not, why?_____

_____

6. Do you have someone in mind to mentor? If yes, please list (maximum: two people). Give name(s), address, E-mail, phone number?
   1. _____
   2. _____

By submitting this application, I agree to fully participate in our organization's pilot mentoring program and attend the training session for mentors. I have discussed the program with my immediate supervisor and received approval to participate. Furthermore, I understand that my participation is contingent upon forming a partnership with a mentee and signing a partnership agreement.

Signed: _____ Date: _____

Prospective Mentor

Pilot Mentoring Program Mentee Application Form

Name:_____ Work phone:_____

Job title: _____ Fax: _____

In company address:_____

E-mail: _____ Work location:_____

Best time/day to be reached:_____

For the information below, use the reverse side or attachment if more space is needed. Please reference item number if you are continuing.

1. Work, educational, and training background (Please include major areas of experience, expertise, etc.):_____
   _____

2. Job experience (List job titles, place employed, and number of years). List only for the last five years: _____
   _____

3. In which areas do you wish to develop your Knowledge, Skills, and Abilities? _____
   _____

4. Please discuss why you wish to be a mentee: _____
   _____

5. Are you willing and able to meet regularly (at least two to four hours a month) with your mentor? (The mentor program committee recommends weekly meetings.)
   Yes _____ No _____ If not, why?_____
   _____

6. Do you have someone in mind to be your mentor? If yes, please identify person and give information on how to contact her or him (Mentees are limited to one mentor for this pilot program.)
   _____
   _____

By submitting this application, I agree to fully participate in our organization's pilot mentoring program and attend the training session for mentees. I have discussed the program with my immediate supervisor and received approval to participate. Furthermore, I understand that my participation is contingent upon forming a partnership with a mentor and signing a partnership agreement.

Signed: _____ Date: _____

Prospective Mentee

STEP 13: SELECT AND NOTIFY PARTICIPANTS, DISTRIBUTE PROJECT INFORMATION AND DESIGN APPRAISALS

When the mentor and mentee application forms are returned, select participants based on criteria consistent with the objectives set for your formal mentoring program, and on the closeness of match with the applicants.

Participants should also be updated on any changed or new information they need, such as whether a mixer will be scheduled and if so, its purpose, process, and where and when it will occur. Even if the matching of pairs are selected by the coordinating team, an opportunity should be arranged so all participants get to know each other in a neutral setting. If the program team matches mentors and mentees, the event might be more formally recognized, such as at a luncheon and short "getting to know you" session. The participants need a chance to interact with their partners and share their backgrounds and experiences that led to this meeting. The use of "ice breaker" exercises for getting to know each other are often used.

At the other end of the selection spectrum is where the participants meet and choose their own partners based on the chemistry of their personalities, personal needs, and developmental needs or interests that often govern the interaction.

For example, the goal of one type of mentoring program is to help new hires adjust and adapt to their new environment and organizational culture. A "buddy" or other partnering term is used as part of induction and orientation process, and interpersonal chemistry may be the deciding factor in the pairings. If, however, the purpose is to help mentees set their specific career goals for the next two to three years, a match can be arranged by the program team based on their expertise and aspirations.

Even when the planning team arranges the match, helping participants break the ice between them is an important factor in how rapidly the relationship begins to bear fruit.

On the following page is a sample worksheet for the design team and the mentoring coordinator to list their ideas about matching methods. The next sheet provides a method for mentors and mentees to express their desires for their prospective partners in greater detail than on the application forms.

DEVELOPING A FORMAL MENTORING PROGRAM
MATCHING MENTORS AND MENTEES

Decide criteria for selecting program mentors:_____

_____

_____

_____

Decide criteria for selecting mentees suitable for this program:_____

_____

_____

_____

Establish criteria for matching mentors and mentees:_____

_____

_____

_____

Decide on techniques/options for deciding quality of the match (such as a personality preference profile, self-selection mixers, etc.) and compatibility of professional fields:_____

_____

_____

_____

Decide how matches will be made (your suggestions):_____

_____

_____

_____

Developing a Formal Mentoring Program
Selecting Mentoring Partners
(For Mentors and Mentees)

Assigning Partners

What kind of a partner would be ideal for you?_____
_____
_____
_____

Your primary reasons for the above:_____
_____
_____
_____

Self-reflection: Do you have any subjective agenda items you are reluctant to share? (Don't necessarily write these down.)

What do you want you and your partner to achieve during the period of the relationship?_____
_____
_____
_____

Prospective [   ] Mentor [   ] Mentee

Name (please type or print):_____

Step 14: The Mixer—A Get Acquainted Session

Having an informal "mixer" is a productive device for organizations that allow mentors and mentees some degree of freedom in choosing their partners. Where mentors and mentees are drawn from different organizational units almost randomly (in contrast to where they share the same type of work or are from the same department) the mixer enables each person to meet their counterparts before forming an alliance. They can check each other out for interpersonal compatibility, common interests, and similar backgrounds and goals. This approach does not suit all situations, but even when the organization or the program administrative personnel actually match mentors and mentees, this kind of social get-together can get each person off to a more comfortable start.

The mixer meeting can be structured in a variety of ways depending on the numbers of participants involved and the best judgment of the design team. Some common options are:

- Have each mentor and mentee write a self-introduction sheet and run off copies they can pass out to potential partners as an interpersonal recruiting tool. This should be a single page, highlighting what each person needs (for the mentee) or has to offer (for the mentor). Job titles for mentors are usually avoided because they can distort the learning process and focus more on competition for acquiring the most prestigious or influential mentors.

- Set up tables with signs telling areas of expertise or interest. Individuals can gather and talk to others with whom they share common interests or needs.

- The use of "icebreaker" techniques or games can introduce participants to everyone involved at least on an elementary level. There are books full of such methods that you can find in libraries or on the Internet. One or two such games can loosen up participants before they start to zero in on likely candidates for partnership. The following coordinator worksheet alerts planners to some of the issues involved in such a meeting.

A GET ACQUAINTED SESSION FOR MENTORS AND MENTEES

Dates and times:_____

Location:_____

Announcement of agenda and format of meeting:_____

_____

Who will arrange these:_____

_____

Planned activities (if any):_____

_____

_____

_____

Get acquainted techniques (if desired, and if so, what):_____

_____

_____

_____

Dress code (if any):_____

Should mentors get together as a group?:_____

_____

Should mentees get together as a group?:_____

_____

If so, before, during or after mixer?:_____

_____

What can you do to develop a supportive group feeling for all mentors
and mentees together?_____

_____

_____

_____

Step 15: Overview Of Program For Participants

There is a broad opportunity for variations in this stage of the program's induction and orientation. However, an hour for each group is minimal. The most common plan involves a two-hour orientation for each group of mentors and mentees.

Details for the program can be dealt with by a broad overview presentation in half an hour, with time allotted for a question and answer session or small group discussion. Most organizations that develop enthusiasm at this stage often build in a demonstration role play session or use a case study of a relationship, followed by small group discussions of the appropriate methods to be used.

Another common variation is to have participants write their questions on three-by-five cards at the end of the first hour. During a short break, the mentoring team's sponsors sort and organize the cards so they can be answered efficiently during the second hour. This approach is much more productive in probing the audience's needs than simply asking "Do you have any questions?"

An effective presentation can also involve the use of audiovisual media to discover attendees learning style preferences.

Some organizations prefer that mentors and mentees be oriented to the program together with their partners in a joint two to three hour session. This approach helps bond each pair closer together, provides grist their mutual discussion of program details, and ensures they both hear the same message.

Content usually includes most of the following subjects, some of which may be repeated during subsequent training to ensure that the basic concepts and practices are grasped.

- A short introduction to the origins of mentoring.
- A definition of the subject.
- What makes mentoring different and special (ie. good, better, best).

- Why the choice of the terms mentor and mentee.
- The evolution from an Industrial Age model to an Information Age model.
- The potential gains to the mentor, mentee, and your organization.

STEP 16: MENTOR SKILLS TRAINING
WARNING—DON'T SKIMP ON TRAINING!

Mentors have been practicing their craft for centuries without any systematic training. But then people have also always been leading others, managing people and things, and supervising workers for the same period of time without any systematic training. A few have done it very well, some wretchedly, and most achieved their purposes somewhere along the spectrum from good to so-so.

Today, few organizations expect their supervisors, managers, and executives (and leaders in each of these categories) to perform at their best without any training; so should it also be for mentors. Mentoring is a key factor in effective leadership and often helps distinguish that category of performance from traditional supervising or managing.

Earlier in this book we looked at many of the aspects of mentoring such as exactly what is mentoring, what makes it different and special, how to move from other helping relationships (such as teaching and tutoring) to adding the mentoring dimension. We even looked at some proposed course content and why those things are important to mentor performance.

When deciding how much training and what kind your course participants should receive, the design team needs to consider three things. First, what will the mentors need to know and be able to do? Second, what role does training and education play in each act, and Third, exactly what Knowledge, Skills, and Abilities (KSAs) will your mentors benefit from applying these to this special relationship.

The science and art of human development is not static—it evolves daily. New techniques and content enter the workplace and training rooms constantly. Sorting through this variable feast can be an exciting challenge. But what are the basics?

Several thousand mentees surveyed over a two-year period who rated their mentors at an "exceptional" level, listed five behaviors that were essential to high performance.

1. He or she listened carefully to what I said (some times took notes) and most often responded to my concerns, ideas, and aspirations item by item.
2. He or she treated our conversations as confidential and with respect, thereby building my trust level.
3. He or she had a strong sense of what was going on in our organization and profession (job field), and helped me develop in helpful ways.
4. He or she encouraged me to take initiatives, explore options, and share my ideas with them and others.
5. He or she helped me to learn new things, solve problems, and even take reasonable chances.

The foregoing items are largely skills, yet are also knowledge based. It has been said, "learning goes best to the teacher." Could striving to help a mentee, develop the mentors so they can also reach higher levels of performance?

Distinguish Between Education and Training

Training and education are so often linked that we may see little or no difference between them. Many programs don't achieve their potential because of a lack of clarity on this point.

Education is acquiring and organizing knowledge and information into useful thought patterns, such as how to solve a problem or play a game. You can choose among the chains of knowledge and know how you have within you to understand, appraise, and decide what to do. We don't always have enough knowledge or use it wisely, so we need to keep acquiring more and organize it better as we go through life. This activity determines our level of wisdom. It is knowledge based, focused on using it for decision-making and determining what we do in different situations, which often constitute the substance of us as a person. It deals with the "why" we do the things we do.

Training is skill and performance based. It centers on doing and relies heavily on learning how we do things, and often requires substantial practice to ensure that we can perform adequately.

Offering mentors only knowledge is like reading a book on how to play golf and then going to a course and expecting to shoot in the low sixties. A program that relies only on training may prepare us very well to respond to a given problem, but if something unexpected and not understood occurs, we may be clueless since we are not equipped to understand why or how something went wrong and what can be done about it. All training courses need a careful balance of each.

A good balance between knowledge and skills produces the ability to understand a problem and move toward resolving it. When you deal with something as complex as helping another person develop their abilities, it is not a "quick fix" situation. This is why the investment in building each mentor's level of effective response may require days rather than minutes or hours.

The suggested training time in this step tends to be minimal and very dependent on the knowledge, skills, and abilities your mentors will bring to the mentoring table. Chapter Four: The Effective Mentor dealt with some traditional behaviors mentors should avoid and Information Age behaviors they should practice. Also briefly discussed were the evolving nature of the roles, relationships, and responsibilities of the mentor. Some of this material should be emphasized in the training of your mentors.

For example, if an organization has in the past only offered soft skills training, such as active listening/reflective feedback techniques to managerial and their professional staff personnel, many of your other mentors may lack these essential skills. If you are planning to do team mentoring, you need considerable mentor educational training and this lack applies to other critical knowledge and skills as well.

However, if confrontation skills, interpersonal problem-solving skills, and envisioning and context shifting are common among your mentors-to-be, the training can be shorter. A close look at your organization's culture, past and future, can help you anticipate the degree and length of training needed. Yet, one common problem in training is likely to remain. Much of mentoring is skill based. Though mentors tend to pass on a great deal of knowledge, concepts, and ideas, how they apply those can be critical.

A major obstacle to effective skills training is the assumption that once a person understands what they are to do and how it is done, they will do it, and well. While we wouldn't assume this in any sport, we should not with mentor skills. Enabling your mentors means considerable practice before competent performance can be assumed. This factor should be included when deciding how much training is enough.

STEP 17: MENTEE SKILLS TRAINING

The whole purpose of mentoring is to enhance the awareness, understanding, and performance of the mentee, yet until quite recently little or no mentee training has been developed. The outcome of the mentoring experience depends on what the mentee chooses to use and do from what they acquire from the relationship. In short, the outcome from a mentoring relationship depends almost entirely on the mentee.

Also, since people who enhance their abilities substantially from the mentoring relationship will in time also become mentors, training mentees constitutes a substantial collective investment in the future of the organization. A day of mentee training is the minimal requirement.

In our organizations, we cannot accept passive, dutiful mentees with limited insight and abilities. Organizations need involved, proactive, creative, potential team leaders who contribute mightily to organizational goals. In today's work teams, leadership gravitates to who or what group has the most effective handle on solving critical issues for their organization. The leadership role often moves on to the person or group who can lead others to the best answers. Well-developed mentees will be the leaders of our future.

This also means a cooperative versus the traditional competitive relationship between individuals and groups. Proactive mentees have become a necessity.

The next page offers a simple but ambitious outline of a typical mentee training program. However, if the training program provides for much participant discussion, a case study or two and some role play for skills development, the course could easily become a two-day workshop.

Chapter 7 identifies a range of typical mentee training modules, some of which you may want to use.

Developing a Formal Mentoring Program
Mentee Skills Development

(One Day)

SESSION I: Being Mentored—A Special Relationship
- Mentoring as a Partnership
- The Mentee's Role and Responsibilities
- Being A Proactive Mentee—Mentors help, Mentees Do!
- Getting In Touch With Your Past Mentoring Experiences
- The Art of Seeking Out Mentors to Help You Identify and Develop Your Talents and Abilities

SESSION II: Becoming An Assertive Learner
- Identifying and Developing Some Key Mentee Skills
- Capturing the Essence of Your Mentor's Assistance
- Internalizing and Using Your Mentor's Help
- The Art of Productive Listening—Workshop Session
- Asking Productive Questions

SESSION III: Making Mentoring Work for You
- Shifting Your Mental Context
- Analyzing Transactions and Using the Discovery
- Method of Self-Development
- Building Trust and Creative Synergy With Your Mentor
- Overcoming Any Self-Imposed Resistance to Change
- Ensuring Balance in Your Working Life

SESSION IV: Mentoring As A Two-Way Street
- Role Models—How to Seek, Access, and Select Them
- Maintaining the Lifelong Process of Personal Development
- Keeping the Relationship Balanced
- Resolving Relationship Problems as Win-Win
- Building Your Personal Network of Mentors

STEP 18: MATCHING MENTORS AND MENTEES

Some organizations prefer to match mentors and mentees just before program launch and others prefer to do it before training so that both groups can experience some of the training together, such as explaining role reationships.

Mentors and their mentees have been getting together informally as long as this practice has been around. A spontaneous connection may not have been the result of any conscious connection—the mentor simply said or did something that another person saw value in, and copied or used it to develop themselves, or used what they absorbed in other important ways.

In recent times, more exact and purposeful transference of knowledge, skills, and abilities are needed, and mentoring relationships have become more organized. These planned "partnerships" require that the matches and how they are arranged need to be done more artfully and with more awareness of the participants needs.

Since these arranged relationships are intended to last for a specific period of time (often for months) and meet specific explicit objectives, great care is required.

However, this matching can occur without any great effort since both partners will have a commitment to work together successfully. Nevertheless, when a bad match occurs for whatever reason, there needs to be a single and virtually neutral method of resolving the relationship.

If both partners are committed to the program, the mentoring coordinator can often arrange other partners for the pair. Having a mentor or mentee in reserve for such situations is often a good idea.

The lists of mentee wants/expectations, characteristics of a good mentor and of mentor wants/expectations, is helpful for participants on both sides of the equation in helping each decide on their own goals.

What Mentees Want/Expect from a Mentor

- Encouragement
- Support
- Honesty
- Candid information and advice
- A "big picture" view of the organization
- Guidance
- Suggestions
- Honest appraisal of capabilities
- Help with grasping the "organizational vision"
- Assistance in making "good" choices
- Information on opportunities, and available assistance in defining and reaching goals
- Benefit of mentor's experiences; what did and did not work
- Understanding of the mentee's abilities and concerns
- Assistance in setting up rotational assignments or cross-training (if appropriate)
- Availability, of time without interruptions
- Non-attribution of sources, honest and open discussions about tough issues
- Assistance in formulating a cohesive development plan
- Help in developing a "network," introduction to other appropriate players
- Idea stimulation, especially insights to career paths and requirements

Characteristics of a Good Mentor

- Supportive
- Patient
- Respected
- People-oriented
- A good encourager/motivator
- Respectful of others
- An effective teacher/trainer
- Self-confident
- An achiever
- One who values the organization and its work

What Mentors Often Want/Expect from a Mentee

- Initiative in revealing their relevant needs and aspirations
- Careful listening
- A focus on solving problems
- Patience
- Candor, honest feedback and discussion
- Clear statements when they don't understand something
- Openness to new ideas
- Willingness to incorporate appropriate changed behaviors
- Alertness to valuable inputs from other sources
- Ability to blend varied ideas into new concepts
- Maintain contact with, and flow of ideas with other mentees in the program
- Willingness to research information on their own
- Punctuality and consistency in attending meetings

Appendix Three:
Program Operation

*I*t used to be that when mentors and mentees had been matched and some training provided (which often was not much), the mentors and their so-called "protégés" began working together. The pair had little guidance except for a vague notion that the mentors were to prepare their neophytes for career success in the same way they had "made it." Mentors made up their activities as they went along, such as mentors teaching "the tricks of the trade" as they had learned them. Sometimes this approach "worked," particularly in organizations that changed little over time. But often much negative information was passed on and wasted time was common. Such training as was offered was most often backward focused rather than forward looking.

"Helping one rise in the organization" is too simplistic and limited for the rapidly advancing Information Age cultures of today. A process of getting to know each other well and sharing of perceptions of each other's abilities, background, and needs leads the partners to develop a functional agenda and a realistic working plan. This saves much time and focuses their energies productively from the beginning.

A workshop session with mentors and mentees to refine their agenda agreements builds each partner's self-confidence. It also produces much more achievement, no matter how long the partnerships are structured to last.

Once the agreement is firm and they begin work in pairs, it is beneficial to have a monthly meeting of all mentors and mentees to discuss and resolve problems and improve their techniques. These people also benefit from supplementary training as suggested by the participants or problem solving meetings when such are necessary.

These activities and assessments of progress by each pair should be made at mid-course, and feed back and corrections (if needed) should be made. This helps ensure maximum achievement, particularly during a pilot program.

On the last day of the program there needs to be an assessment session for even routine (not pilot) programs to detect changes or embellishments of the program.

See appropriate steps for sample assessment forms.

STEP 19: OFFICIAL LAUNCH OF THE FORMAL MENTORING PROGRAM

When your organization is about to start the first interaction of participants in a sponsored mentoring program (or the pilot program) the official launch is more than the calendar date when the mentors and mentees start working together.

The "launch" is official recognition of a major event in the employer's employee development efforts. It is also a chance for major publicity for the program itself and marketing the ideas of mentoring to the organization-wide population, and possibly even to the community beyond the organization's walls.

Such publicity also increases the program's public profile and may encourage personnel in other segments of the organization to launch complementary programs.

For instance, in hospitals it is quite common to have a variety of ongoing mentoring programs, formal and informal, in a variety of technical and professional disciplines. Trading ideas, experience, and resources between them creates considerable synergy for the benefit of the overall organization.

The mentoring program team may also want to brainstorm other avenues of employee and public awareness.

Following is a typical letter for internal broadcast. Adapt this letter to suit your needs and goals, or design your own announcement, but it should not be too long, too detailed, or too complex.

INTERNAL NOTICE OF OFFICIAL PROGRAM LAUNCH (SAMPLE)

Company logo here

Company name
Address
Date:

To:

Today the Human Resources Department is launching a six-month pilot mentoring program for new employees. The goal is to improve retention of new employees and to assist new hires in adapting successfully to their new workplace; become oriented more quickly to our organization and its goals, visions, and culture, and help them assess their personal work and professional aspirations within our organization.

Volunteer employee mentors have received training in how to practice the craft of mentoring. Those individuals being mentored, our mentees, have received training in "how to make the most of being mentored." When this pilot is complete, we anticipate refining the program and offering it periodically to other new people as they enter the company.

In fairness to all, participation in this program will offer no special advantage in career advancement over other employees. We encourage seasoned employees to volunteer to serve as mentors in future repeats of this program.

Signed

Press Release
Public Notice of Offical Program Launch (Sample)

Date:

Today the XYZ Company is launching a six-month pilot formal mentoring program for new employees. The goal is to assist all new hires adapt successfully to their new workplace, become oriented more quickly to our organization's goals, visions, and culture, as well as to receive information, guidance, and help that each person needs to achieve their work and professional aspirations.

Volunteer employee mentors have received training in how to practice the craft of mentoring. Those individuals seeking to be so mentored have also received training in how to make the most of being mentored. When this pilot program is complete, we will refine the program and offer it to other new employees who volunteer to participate.

Participation in this program offers no advantage in career advancement over other employees, except as each person chooses to apply the lessons learned in their daily tasks. This program is offered by our company to uncover employee talents, drive, and diverse interests with the aim of creating a more family like enviornment for our workforce.

Signed

Note: It is important that each organization design their own announcement to fit organizational realities and goals. The program task force and coordinator should check the announcement with the human resources manager and possibly their legal staff, if they decide to publicly announce the launch of their program. Also, the nature of internal and/or external organizational distributions should be studied.

Step 20: Initial Working Meeting
of Mentor and Mentee Pairs

The most successful formal mentoring programs rest on a solid foundation of partnership between mentor and mentee. This is where open communication, mutual respect, and trust flourish so that a genuine concern for each other develops as the partnership evolves.

To reach its full potential, mentoring requires the creation of unusual events or circumstances by the mentor, as well as uncommon involvement in learning processes by the mentee. The mentor may search for unusual learning opportunities and experiences for their mentee. Mentees may supplement the mentor's help by studying a subject the mentor is helping them with, to greater depths and from diverse viewpoints to enlarge their understanding of the lessons offered.

The relationship must occur in a risk-free environment where each person can take initiative and even some risks to achieve superior results. However, to avoid going overboard in the realm of risk or damaging the relationship they must, early on, set some mutual parameters within which they agree to work.

Some expectations may not be met. Good faith in working together is essential. At this point the partners might share with each other their ideas about what their mentoring agreement might contain and list their ideas for that discussion.

If two people are to work as true "partners" in a formal mentoring relationship it is imperative they share their expectations with each other. This is where differences in rank, position power, and personal influence can create the "awe factor" for the mentee. On the other hand, this awe can lead to discounting the mentee's needs or build other barriers between the partners. A candid initial statement from each person can be very helpful, such as: "This is what I hope to gain/achieve from this relationship in the next few weeks (or months)."

After this initial period, the partners may want to firm up or alter their expectations. If you are willing to update your expectations, write them here:_____

_____

_____

The mentee can also write one or more statements such as those below (or discuss them verbally), and anything else she or he may be willing to share:_____

_____

_____

I have set the following development plans that I want to achieve in the next few weeks or months:_____

_____

_____

_____

I need to know more about:_____

_____

_____

I want to strengthen the following skills:_____

_____

_____

I think you need to know this about me (For this last item, a discussion may be preferable to a written statement.):_____

_____

_____

_____

THINGS WE NEED TO AGREE ON

Our goals must be mutual or at least compatible—are they?_____

_____

Is the relationship based on a sense of mutual respect and equality? If not, why not? And if not, what can we do about this?____

_____

_____

_____

Is the relationship to be truly punishment and judgment-free? Is the mentee expected to take some risk and show initiative?_____

_____

_____

_____

How do we make the above explicit to our partner?_____

_____

_____

_____

_____

GETTING ORGANIZED—MEETING LOGISTICS

The most productive meetings in a formal mentoring relationship are short and frequent, an hour or two a week, often combined with an at-work break or lunch. Logistics are usually mutually decided during the first meeting. A working agenda topics to be discussed, usually made up by the mentee) is common. Yet either partner can offer an agenda item, such as:

How often will we meet?_____

_____

_____

Where will we meet?_____

_____

_____

How long will our meetings usually last?_____

_____

_____

What days of the week (or the month) will we meet?_____

_____

If it is necessary to cancel or change a time or place of a meeting, how will we handle that?_____

_____

GETTING ORGANIZED—MEETING LOGISTICS

Who will be responsible for setting each meeting agenda?_____
_____

What time of the day will we meet?_____
_____

How can we best contact each other?_____
_____

How do we alter this arrangement if it became necessary?_____
_____

Mentors numbers
Office phone:_____
Cell phone:_____
Fax:_____
E-mail:_____

Mentees numbers
Office phone:_____
Cell phone:_____
Fax:_____
E-mail:_____

Other items that need attention:_____

STEP 21: DEVELOPING A TENTATIVE AGREEMENTS

One or both partners can push the mentor/mentee partnership agreement. For example, the mentor knows a great deal about the program—its goals and objectives—while the mentee is only somewhat aware of what she or he doesn't know about the area of work they are preparing to tackle (such as learning a government agency's contracting system). On launch date or soon after the partners need to share a great deal of information with each other about themselves, and also about any doubts, uncertainties, and feelings they may have about the program.

By this stage both people have some ideas about what they need or can give in the relationship. Yet, it has been found that in the early sessions of the relationship, both mentors and mentees are overly optimistic as to what can be achieved. This implies that some reality checks will be helpful.

The following forms are suggestions and will need to be modified by the mentoring task force to meet your program needs. Many adjustments between mentor and mentee may affect the sequencing of a particular kind of help. For example, the need for possible referral of the mentee to other people resources. Also, the effects of external events such as the changing of work schedules of the participants may require adjustments. However, a general plan as well as a general agreement can be produced in this meeting and can be refined and expanded in Step 22.

Developing a Mentor/Mentee Partnership Agreement

Message to My Mentee:_____
_____

Is there anything I can do to ensure that we start well together?
_____
_____

What can I do to increase the comfort level between us?_____
_____
_____

Is there anything I should know about you early in our relationship, such as preferences, strengths/needs, likes/dislikes?_____
_____
_____

What is your preferred method of learning, observing, listening, hands-on, graphs, charts?_____
_____
_____

What is the most important thing you would like to get from our relationship?_____
_____

What developmental needs, skills, knowledge, and abilities, will be most valued by you from this relationship?_____
_____

What else is important to you?_____
_____
_____

Mentor/Mentee Partnership Agreement

Message to my mentor:_____
_____
_____

I need to know more about:_____
_____
_____

I would like to strengthen these particular skills:_____
_____
_____

I have set the following personal development plans for myself, to be achieved during our time together:_____
_____
_____
_____

I think you need to know this about me (you may prefer to discuss this item personally):_____
_____
_____
_____

Miscellaneous?_____
_____
_____

Specific Initial Objective or Plans

As Mentor:_____

_____

_____

I would appreciate the following types of assistance or support
from the mentoring coordinator:_____

_____

I need the following help to move the mentoring process along:

_____

_____

My specific initial objectives:_____

_____

_____

As Mentee:_____

_____

I would appreciate the following types of assistance or support
from the mentoring coordinator:_____

_____

_____

I need the following help to move the mentoring process along:

_____

_____

My specific initial objectives:

_____

Step 22: Workshop Session to Finalize Mentor-Mentee Agreements

Developing a realistic, challenging, but workable mentoring agreement is at the crux of a successful program.

This workshop should precede the ongoing working meeting of the mentor and mentee pairs so they can be trained in how to develop a quality agreement. Otherwise, such an approach often leads to a set of common, canned statements where most or all of the agreements tend to sound alike. This can be effective in some ways, but runs the risk of failing to take advantage of each mentor's uniqueness and the particular experience and the personalization brought on by the character background and special needs of each mentee. Judge for yourself, but recognize the following:

"You and I may have worked for the same organization for the same number of years and do the same type of work. Yet my feelings about that work, my accomplishments (or the lack of them), my particular insights and conclusion about it, and my view of the future is quite different from yours."

Also (for example), each mentee will have her or his special needs, aspirations, and hopes for this new way of doing things. That person also has their self-beliefs about themselves and their strengths and weaknesses (which may or may not be accurate).

To the degree that such things are personal, different, and inhibiting of each of us, it sometimes takes getting to know the other person by working on an agreement first to discover what pitfalls are possible.

Factors to be considered:
- The complexity of the program's objectives.
- The amount and quality of the skills training given to each of the partners.
- The duration of the program.
- The developmental goals for the mentee.
- The relevance of the mentor's experience and know-how in the subject matter to be transferred (and any number of other considerations). A workshop for the partners to refine their tentative agreements makes especially good sense in a pilot program.

Ask each pair to share the nature of their agreement in a group of mentors and mentees. The discussion of the different agreements is a bit risky, but often can be highly productive.

Ask the partners to identify their uncertainties before the workshop so that a consultant or the design team can explore their problems, as the workshop agenda unfolds. This has proved beneficial in many cases, especially where the mentoring was planned to explore non-traditional areas of options or new aspects of organizational development.

Some organizations also ask participants to send in their tentative agreements for analysis and consultation by a design team member or a mentoring consultant. But such partners may miss the value of larger group interchange, which can be a broadening experience and often prepare participants for engaging in other mentoring efforts beyond this pilot.

The goal of this session is to establish a reasonable but challenging program for each pair of partners to achieve by the end of their formal relationship.

Mentoring management team members can usually play a constructive role in the design and operation of this workshop.

STEP 23: REGULAR MENTOR/MENTEE MEETINGS

Regular and frequent meetings between partners will continue interest at a high and consistent level. This often means the partner breaking their objectives into reasonable, bite-size chunks so that some degree of achievement can be shared and enjoyed at each meeting, to the greatest degree possible.

Every mentor/mentee meeting should be carefully planned so as to be productive. This is often best accomplished by stating one or two specific "outcome objectives" for that meeting.

The typical "tick list" agenda where several things to be discussed are jotted down by one or both partners, may work, but that approach often leads to a wandering discussion with nothing decided or accomplished.

A typical example of the agenda item "tick list" might be:
1. Employee assistance program
2. Leave policy and practice.
3. Human resources person in Building 3.

A more focused set of "outcome objectives" from a mentee's perspective might be:
1. Gain exact knowledge of each employee assistance program benefit service offered by our company to our employees.
2. Have a concise statements of an employee leave policy as it applies to me—now.
3. Be introduced to the human resources person in Building 3 by my mentor and ask her for a tour of those facilities at her convenience.

Ask yourself (and your mentor or mentee) what did we accomplish during this meeting?

The weekly (bi-weekly, or monthly) mentor/mentee meeting should achieve one or more specific steps during that calendar period. The partners should share the specifics of achievement, or the lack of them. Don't settle for vague indefinite statements, nor should worthy objectives necessarily be dropped because new ones are added. Apply imagination and creative problem solving to overcome any slippage.

Stopping each meeting on time is important, but not an absolute if other factors interfere with scheduled accomplishments. However, it works best if the partners focus on solving such problems so that consistency of progress is achieved.

Sometimes changes in circumstances require shift from old to new objectives. Objectives can diminish in importance, some be elevated to enhanced concern. Below are some subjective signs of a successful mentoring relationship and its maintenance. Each person should review these factors from time to time individually or as partners, to see if rough spots exist or are developing that need problem solving.

- Both parties are enthusiastic, even inspired.
- The partners experience a growing bond or connection between them.
- They are able to establish a comfortable environment for discussion and learning.
- The mentee is open to personal change and development.
- The mentor searches for new insights and novel ways to share his or her experience and expertise.
- The mentee searches for better ways to internalize, remember, and apply what they are learning.
- The mentor searches for, and shows their partner new aspects of the mentee's potential.
- Each partner commits to expanding his or her own personal learning and understanding from the relationship.
- Both are willing to seek, share, and include new learning in the partnership.

- When the program is over and/or the time comes to separate, the relationship is balanced and friendly.
- Both may agree to continue the relationship on an informal as needed basis.

STEP 24: MONTHLY TRAINING AND/OR PROBLEM-SOLVING MEETINGS

Organizations that sponsor formal mentoring programs for specific periods of time, often find it useful to hold short, monthly meetings of mentor and mentee pairs as a group get-together. This is particularly common with pilot programs.

Reserve the first, or first few, of these monthly meetings for sharing problems, achievements, and solutions to problems among partners and in larger group as appropriate. The program consultant or other experts can also be engaged to provide supplemental training to reinforce or expand mentee and/or mentor skills.

These monthly meetings ensure program momentum, strengthen relationships, enable participant networking for special expertise, and improve the quality of partner interactions. Mentor/mentee suggestions for training exercises, subject matter lectures, or other inputs often contribute to a stimulating program.

List any ideas you might have for such meetings:

_____

_____

_____

_____

_____

_____

_____

_____

_____

Some organizations offer other short training or development programs outside the above monthly meetings of value to mentoring pairs. Please list any thoughts you have for such experiences:_____

_____

_____

_____

_____

Many mentoring sponsoring groups also plan periodic mentoring activities or training sessions to supplement their prior formal skills training to help their participant partners enhance their relationship. When this is done in a pilot program, it is a good idea to design a special assessment instrument to get feedback on how useful each is to the mentoring task. Trainees usually rate these supplementary training sessions very highly. Some of the most popular and effective ones are:

- The Myers–Briggs Personality Profile Indicator (with participant sharing exercises)
- How to deliver and effective "I" message confrontation
- How to make your active listening/reflective feedback techniques more effective
- The Howard Gardner's "seven flavors of genius"– developing awareness of diverse inner strengthism each person
- New perspectives on motivation
- Building interpersonal trust and confidence
- Evolving models of organization and how to adjust to them
- Careers of the future–how to help your mentee prepare
- How to expand your mentoring network
- How to participate in and support mentoring efforts in your community
- How to move from mentee to mentor

Survey your own program participants for additional ideas.

STEP 25: MONTHLY MEETINGS OF ALL MENTORS AND MENTEES AND PROGRAM PROGRESS ASSESSMENT

Many successful pilot programs schedule a once a month meeting of all mentors and mentees with the partners setting their own agenda and managing their meeting for one or all of the following reasons:

1. To refresh the partners and help them discuss among themselves issues and answers to questions that have arisen in the program and in their relationships.
2. To share mentoring tools or techniques the mentors/ mentees have found to be especially helpful.
3. To share new ideas and sources of help that become available.
4. To fill out and discuss each mentor's or mentee's monthly assessment sheets.
5. To discuss new issues that arise with a focus on problem solving.
6. To focus on problem solving or improving partner performance.
7. Anything else that seems worthwhile to discuss.

STEP 26: PROGRAM COORDINATOR PROVIDES ASSESSMENT FORMS

Midpoint assessment of progress is particularly important for pilot programs since they can lead to program improvements and to a final assessment of such changes in the program. Assessment at other points may also be helpful. Sample assessement forms are included for your consideration. Modify as needed.

When conducting a pilot program, many organizations assign a personal identification number (PIN) to each mentor/mentee pair and sends them a confidential monthly assessment form that is returned to the mentoring coordinator.

The pin number enables the coordinator to contact any individual if additional information or clarification is needed. The coordinator may also arrange counseling services for that individual to resolve a relationship or other problem.

However, the primary purpose of the assessment is gather information on group results and make project adjustments as needed.

The length of time the pilot program lasts influences whether other interim assessments are needed. Unless something drastic occurs, the mid-point assessment works well for three to six-month pilot programs.

The forms are collected at the joint monthly meeting of all mentors and mentees. Modify the following forms as needed for your program. They can be used without the pin numbers, but confidentiality should be respected.

Mentor Monthly Assessment Form
(use back if more space is needed)

Mentoring team personal identification number (PIN): _____

Month:_____

Highlights:_____

Tasks accomplished as projected:_____

_____

Variations from scheduled activities:_____

_____

Lessons from these variations:_____

_____

Modifications or adjustments:_____

_____

Comments:_____

_____

_____

_____

_____

_____

_____

_____

_____

_____

_____

_____

_____

_____

_____

_____

MENTEE MONTHLY ASSESSMENT FORM
(use back if more space is needed)

Mentoring team personal identification number (PIN): _____

Month:_____

Highlights:_____

Tasks accomplished as projected:_____

_____

Variations from scheduled activities:_____

_____

Lessons from these variations:_____

_____

Modifications or adjustments:_____

_____

Comments:_____

_____

_____

_____

_____

_____

_____

_____

_____

_____

_____

_____

_____

_____

The Mentoring Organization

MENTORING PROGRAM MID-COURSE
ASSESSMENT AND POSSIBLE CORRECTION

I served as a:
Mentor:_____ Mentee:_____ in this experience. Team PIN:_____

Please describe one to three important developments that have occurred to you in this relationship.

1._____
2._____
3._____

I would personally rate this program as:
- ❑ A great success
- ❑ Valuable
- ❑ Satisfactory
- ❑ Of little or no value

Comments (continue on back if necessary):_____

_____
_____
_____
_____
_____
_____
_____
_____
_____
_____
_____

REVIEW OF THE MENTORING EXPERICENCE AND SUGGESTIONS

Mentoring Team PIN_____

Please check appropriate box   MENTOR ❐ MENTEE ❐

What can be done by the organization to enhance this experience?_____
_____
_____
_____

What could I have done to enhance my own experience?_____
_____
_____
_____
_____

What could my group (mentors or mentees) have done as a group
to enhance this experience?_____
_____
_____
_____

Suggestions for improving future programs:_____
_____
_____
_____

REVIEW OF MENTORING EXPERIENCE

Anonymous Personal Experience
Please check appropriate box   MENTOR ☐   MENTEE ☐

PRO

_____

_____

_____

_____

_____

_____

_____

_____

_____

_____

CON

_____

_____

_____

_____

_____

_____

_____

_____

_____

_____

_____

STEP 27: MID-COURSE ASSESSMENT REPORT
AND POSSIBLE CORRECTION

You can get an early look at how your program is developing from the mentoring coordinator's mid-course report. The mentoring program coordinator will summarize the results and make suggestions. The program management team often will determine if structural changes should be made at this point. If things look good, wait until the final assessment and your final report on this (pilot) program before making changes that will prevail with your next mentoring group.

The forms used to collect the data have been used successfully by many organizations. Some modified them to provide greater depth, especially where professional mentoring, i.e., financial, engineering, or scientific pairs, were working together.

The need for such changes should be viewed as an opportunity rather than as criticism or a failure. The goal is not so much to evaluate, but to improve the quality of the relationships from now to the end of this group's activities.

For instance, you may be able to add some needed skills training for the group during one of the monthly meetings. For instance, training to improve the mentors' performance can be given to the mentors at one of the monthly meetings while the mentees are doing something else. Or, since most mentees will in time become mentors; possibly both groups could be trained in the same thing at the same time.

STEP 28: CONTINUED REGULAR MEETINGS

Unless the mid-course assessment signals a need for change, or other important modifications are required, the rest of the program consists of maintenance and support while the monthly reports are gathered and analyzed.

The main things we've seen happen during this period tend to be few (as listed below) but of considerable importance to the individuals involved.

- *A souring of the relationship between a pair of partners.* Expert counseling was able to solve most such problems. If that didn't work, a "no fault" divorce was arranged (even if one or both partners thought fault was involved).

- *One of the partners left the organization.* Curiously, in most cases the relationship was able to continue until the end of the program, even when conducted by E-mail, telephone, or fax. This happened most often when the partners had developed a commitment to each other. We also found that while some of the agreement items had to be modified, few items were dropped.

- *A significant job change occurred to one of the partners.* This radically changed the nature of the agreement; left the person with no time to continue to meet. In several cases a new mentor or mentee was found if the partnership had not gone too far toward completion. If it had, the pair declared "victory" and parted.

- *Sometimes a poor match was noted.* Usually this surfaced early and other more compatible partners were found. In cases where this couldn't be done, the partners left the program. The most common reason for this-with the mentor-was unsuitability for the role (such as a domineering personality), or—with the mentee—took intractable positions usually demanding something which by design was outside of the program's parameters, such as "guaranteed advancement." This sort of problem oc curred in less than one percent of the programs we've assisted in establishing. Initial screening of participants usually avoided this hazard.

- *The partners lagged behind in achieving their own scheduled objectives.* Often this was because they had stretched themselves too far in the beginning or other job demands intruded on the time of one or both of them. The mentoring team was most often able to help them reach a reasonable compromise to solidify their achievements or extend the duration of the relationship. In the case of a pilot program, the cause of the missed objectives was often factored into program design of future iterations.

Step 29: Final Assessment Session—End of Program

Since a mentoring relationship is a joint venture between a mentee and a mentor, this assessment at the end of the program should be done together. If both partners have been straight with each other, there should be little disagreement between them.

Most organizations we have worked with held a meeting of the whole group at the program's conclusion, and after some general discussion allowed each pair to answer the assessment sheets together.

Attached are two sample forms commonly used for this purpose. Again, adapt them to your needs and goals.

First, each team should develop testimonials they agree were accomplishments of activities they consider noteworthy or even exciting achievements. The back of the testimonial sheet can be used for expansion.

Second, the end of mentoring assessment sheets cover only the major objectives or a great number of them if that was the result of your experience. Where the participants are reporting on a pilot program, the answers are particularly important for collectively they provide the basis for improving future iterations of your organization's mentoring program.

TESTIMONIALS

Mentoring team:_____

Describe accomplishment or activity that mentor and mentee wish
to share:_____

_____

_____

_____

_____

_____

_____

_____

_____

_____

_____

_____

_____

_____

_____

_____

_____

_____

_____

_____

_____

_____

_____

End of Mentoring Program Assessment Sheet

Mentoring team:_____

List original objectives and assign a completion grade of A, B, C, D or F (not dealt with).

Objective   Grade

1._____ _____

2._____ _____

3._____ _____

4._____ _____

5._____ _____

For any objective graded below a B, please explain what impeded higher performance.

Objective:_____

_____

Objective:_____

_____

Objective:_____

_____

For any objective graded A or B assess cause for success.

Objective:_____

_____

Objective:_____

_____

Objective:_____

_____

Identify key factors contributing to positive outcomes.

_____

_____

Identify key factors that impeded or limited greatest possible performance. _____

_____

_____

_____

How often did mentoring team meet and was that adequate or inadequate?_____

_____

_____

_____

Where and under what circumstances did meetings occur?

_____

_____

_____

_____

What discernible impact has the mentoring experience had on your performance and professional prospects?_____

_____

_____

_____

_____

Additional comments:_____

_____

_____

_____

_____

_____

_____

Appendix Four:
Preparation for Next
Iteration of the Program

*I*t may be "all over but the shouting," but many organizations offer some sort of celebration for the participants and the program staff. This is often a type of "commencement party" or reception to celebrate a new phase in their work career which will include mentoring, and the end of the preparation for it.

Now that the mentors have been well trained, possess greater knowledge and skills in the art of people development, and have demonstrated their newfound competence successfully, they can now mentor widely in the organization, and possibly outside it as well.

The mentees will be more self-assertive in defining, articulating, and seeking help within the organization, and pursue their own self-managed careers and personal aims. Also, they now possess more skills for ingesting, organizing, and using the skills and knowledge they need for their career (and even lifelong) learning. They should recognize they are now part of a larger organizational web of resource people who may become mentors themselves.

This is often considered cause for celebration and additional publicity concerning mentoring itself. Yet, there is still much work to be done by the program's staff.

The results from the final assessment session and the learning gained from earlier assessments and summaries of participant experience needs to be assembled, organized, and reported in a final document. Even if for economic or other reasons, the decision is made to not continue additional mentoring programs, the learning gained from this program, in this environment, and at this time should not be lost from the organizational memory.

More often though, other informal or formal programs will spring from these seeds and they will benefit from the lessons learned from your program. Many times more ideal, productive, and even challenging programs will be sanctioned so that the model can be amended as appropriate to ensure even greater success.

Program changes should be made soon after the conclusion of the pilot so that earlier comments by participants and staff can be checked with their originators before such people are too dispersed and their reasons forgotten. Much can be gained if preparation for the next iteration of the program begins almost immediately so that momentum is not lost.

STEP 30: PARTICIPANT CELEBRATION

When a formal mentoring program concludes there is generally a sense of euphoria, shared good feelings toward their counterparts, and enthusiasm for future mentoring work with new partners for the mentors, and an eagerness to continue applying what they have learned for the mentees.

It is also common for the mentees in any such program to consider acting as mentors to other people in the organization whom they believe they can help. For example, they may act as mentors in informal relationships with coworkers, in their own family, or in their communities as volunteers.

It is not surprising that many of the participants want to celebrate their recent experience in some fashion. The employing organization usually finances such a celebration.

We have witnessed such celebrations where participants and the managing team members, read from their testimonial sheets, or "witness" as to ways the experience has or is expected to enhance their abilities. Examples are given as to how they have been changed by the experience, new perceptions of their organization, and the effects the program has had on their relationships with their work mates.

Often the mentors felt as strongly as their mentees about the experience. When finished with their assessments, some groups have also enjoyed a social period where refreshments were provided by their organization. In another scenario, the employing organization hosted a luncheon at a first-class restaurant with speakers—speeches and perhaps special guests.

The bonds cemented between participants at such a celebration will be memorable when a pilot program has been undertaken and may signal the dawn of a mentoring culture in the organization.

Step 31: Writing and Submission of Final Report

In a pilot program, this provides the basis for changes in the program that can improve performance in future programs.

It is important to consider having members of the design, development, and implementation teams participate and/or contribute to the final report, especially the recommendations segment.

The periodic assessment sheets, mid-course assessment, and feedback from the partners should be used to back up recommendations for program improvement. The recommendations for modifications and improvement are usually the most critical portion of the report and should stand out clearly and boldly.

Let us hope that all changes will be beneficial and serve your organization and its people well.

STEP 32: AMEND THE PROGRAM PLAN AS APPROPRIATE

The chances are excellent that you have had a successful program with only minor adjustments needed, yet in the spirit of "continuous improvement" plans for expansion, refinement, or enhancement are always possible. Every useful option should be explored.

STEP 33: BEGIN PREPARATIONS FOR THE NEXT PROGRAM

Start at the beginning for the next group and the next program.

OTHER SOURCES

*F*or those who want a broader and deeper background on the development and practice of mentoring the following works are suggested for your consideration.

THE CLASSICS

The Odyssey by Homer, translated by Samuel Butler (New York, NY: Barnes and Noble Books, New York 1993)

There are several excellent translations of Homer's book that tells the story of mentor, the tale which gave mentoring its name and essence. But I prefer Butler's version for its clarity and organization, and the fact that it has been available in hardback as well as soft. There are actually two stories in *The Odyssey*—that of Ulysses' travels and the one that concerns his family and mentor. The later is a fascinating story of loyalty, trust, and personal development well worth reading for its own sake.

Mentoring Relationships—How They Aid Creative Achievement, Endure, Change, and Die by E. Paul Torrance (Buffalo, NY: Bearly Limited Press, Buffalo, New York 1984)

Torrance reports on the first detailed study of the effects of mentoring on a given population, in this case on school children.

He also follows them from their early schooling into adulthood. In his later works, he sought information on similar mentoring experiences in other countries and cultures. Many of his observations were insightful and helped to shape the use of mentoring in many organizations to this day.

Unfortunately, he made some (I believe unnecessary and inaccurate) negative statements about young women being mentored. Ironically, those comments were made when some of the greatest advances in mentoring were being made by and for women.

From the early 1970s, networking to provide (among other things) systematic, mentoring help to and among women, advanced this people development art enormously. For instance, it opened mentoring to the idea of using a network of multiple mentors to work with multiple mentees on an "as needed" basis instead of just one-on-one. Also, these women focused on the idea of helping a person develop a total personal and flexible career plan rather than just focusing on how to succeed in a specific organization. These women also taught each other a variety of new mentoring skills and substantially advanced the concept of the value of diversity in the work place.

Mentoring At Work—Developmental Relationships in Organizational Life by Kathy E Kram (Glenview, IL: Scott, Foresman and Company, Glenview, IL 1985)

This was, in many ways, the first book that offered a comprehensive analysis, description, and thoughtful projection on the art of mentoring, up to that time. She said: "I discuss a perspective on mentoring I hope will discourage the 'search for the right mentor' and encourage systematic self-diagnosis of relationship needs, as well as strategies for building relationships that provide relevant developmental functions."

Kram also developed ideas on the psychosocial functions as well as the career functions of mentoring; phases of the relationship;

the complexities of cross-gender relationships and peer relationships (including the factors of individual and organizational differences); and creating conditioning that encouraged the use of mentoring. This systematic study of mentoring laid the groundwork for understanding the evolutionary nature of the art.

THE MIDDLE PERIOD

In the 1980s and 1990s, several substantial mentoring works appeared which tended to sharply focus on career development as used in the tall hierarchal organizations of that time. There was also some research-based material on other growing interests in mentoring, such as its use in academic environments and in meeting community needs. The following are the ones I considered the best of that period.

The Mentor Connection by Michael G. Zey (New York, NY: Dow Jones - Irwin, New York, 1984)

In his preface Zey lays out his premise early: This book looks at the ways that connecting with a mentor effects people's careers, increases their chances of success and enhances the quality of their work life. A mentor, a senior person in an organization who oversees the development and progress of a junior person, a protégé, can have a powerful effect on the junior person's career." This sums up the elitist essence of Industrial Age Mentoring which has largely been outdated with the downsizing and delayering of the old hierarchical organization. As the personal computer appeared on nearly every desk, giving instant access to nearly all business transactions, the use of Information systems and the creation of new more democratic corporate cultures, this approach to mentoring faded.

Yet, there are many provocative questions and some interesting idea nuggets in Zey's work that are otherwise likely to be lost because of its archaic thesis.

The collected works of Dr. Norman H. Cohen, all published by HRD Press of Amhurst, MA, most in the late 1990s, such as:
- *Effective Mentoring*
- *The Principles of Adult Mentoring Inventory*
- *The Mentees Guide to Mentoring*
- *The Managers Pocket Guide to Mentoring*

These books advance the work of Zey and suffer somewhat by the same narrowness of focus on Organizational Mentoring.

Dr. Cohen writes in an academic style, but also makes a major effort "to offer concise practical guidance to mentors and mentees." His materials tend to be very thorough and extremely well developed in great detail. His works also offer another viewpoint on how to train and develop mentoring partners and on ways to set up a mentoring program. His production of works on Mentoring subjects is continuing.

Managers as Mentors by Chip Bell (San Francisco, CA: Berrett–Koehler Publishers, San Francisco, 1996)

I believe that this is the best written of the Industrial Age books on Mentoring and it contains many interesting stories and anecdotes that Chip uses to make his points.

Though it struggles to reflect the leading edge of knowledge and skills of the "learning organization" it still is top down i.e.: it consentrates on the successful achiever, orientations in the stereotypical hierarchical organization and even used that terrible "P" word - protégé. Its very title builds a fence around the book and though he struggles to create a sense of partnership and awareness of the changes occurring in managee/subordinates relationship they don't always shine through.

In total, though, there is much to recommend this book and most of his forward looking stuff is "right on." I consider this the best of the old school works, and it is full of some good ideas (particularly in the communications aspects of the art) for the reader to uncover.

INFORMATION AGE MENTORING

The 1980s and 1990s also saw a great growth in the realm of conscious, systematic, and democratic mentoring across almost all sectors of society.

It can easily be claimed that people in almost any walk of life or situation can acquire the help of a mentor and/or be exposed to a mentoring program and even receive training as a mentor (or even as a mentee).

For example academic mentoring has spread from the college campus into the grades K-12 with students mentoring other students and teachers: mentoring less experienced teachers as well as acting in their usual role as informal or situational mentors to students displaying special talents or needs.

Also community mentoring by neighborhood volunteers through local churches, community centers, and school programs has become quite common. Often such programs have become more systematic and skill based in giving assistance to poor, disadvantaged, and at risk students, and potential school dropouts. Likewise, mentoring has become common in programs as disparate as with: helping prisoners and addicted people and in supporting "welfare to work" programs. Today there are few areas in the U.S., at least, where conscious mentoring assistance is not being offered by someone or some group.

Many local governments at the city, county, state, or federal level also have available some type of training manual and or program, for (at least) informal mentor's. You may want to check local resources for what might be available in your area.

One of my favorites of these is listed below:

- *The Two Of Us—a Handbook for Mentors*, by Marilyn W. Smith and published by The Abell Foundation of Baltimore, MD. This and other materials on mentoring are now available through The Maryland Mentoring Partnership, 517 N. Charles St., Suite 200, Baltimore, MD, 21201.

This work covers just about everything imaginable for helping youth receive: encouragement, increased self-awareness and respect, help with planning their future, and various developmental gains. This book also includes a host of exercises and activities mentors can use to provide assistance and growth experiences to those youths, whom they volunteer in their communities.

Mentors—Making a Difference in Our Public Schools, by Thomas W. Evans (Princeton, NJ: Peterson's Guides, Princeton, NJ, 1992)

I believe that this is the first Information Age book I have read. I have not seen one quite like it. It begins on a grand theme —Mentors (who are) Making (or attempting to make) a constructive Difference In Our Public Schools. He makes his case for such a need very well. Then he collects a variety vignettes under a number of general topics such as: Working from the Inside (of the System); "Adopt A School" is Alive and Well; Start Your Own Organization; Creating a New School; Transforming a City (and the State System); and How You Can Make a Difference. Each section contains stories of several people who made an important difference in student's lives and in improving their schooling in some fashion or another through the efforts of these "Mentors."

Overall, Evans makes the important point that it is usually through the efforts of individuals, and then through groups, working from the bottom up (rather than from the top down) that innovative and practical answers are generated. The fact that the advances he documents have moved on since the book was published is not too important since Evans' purpose was to illustrate and inspire rather than to prescribe.

ABOUT THE AUTHOR

Gordon F. Shea serves as president of PRIME Systems Company, a training, consulting, and human resource development firm in the Washington–Baltimore area. Prior to launching his own firm, he worked as a supervisor, manager, and executive in government and private industry for 25 years. Mr. Shea earned degrees from Syracuse University and George Washington University.

Beginning his career as a technical writer and industrial engineer, he climbed the ranks in corporations such as Honeywell and Litton Industries, eventually becoming vice president of engineering for a broad-based management consulting firm.

Mr. Shea's over 500 training and consulting clients include corporations such as IBM, Exxon, and General Electric; associations such as APPA (Association of Higher Education Physical Plant Administrators); governmental agencies such as the National Aeronautics and Space Administration (NASA), the National Institute of Health, and the United States Departments of Transportation, Defense, and Agriculture; professional associations such as the National Association of Media Executives; and major universities such as Cornell, Georgetown, and the University of Pennsylvania.

Mr. Shea is author or co-author of sixteen books on management, leadership, communications, and corporate cultures, and four works on mentoring. His Crisp Publications books *Mentoring—How to Develop Successful Mentor Behaviors*, (for mentors), and *Making the Most of Being Mentored*, (for mentees), provide complementary skills training for participants in mentoring training courses. Mr. Shea also contributed the chapter on mentoring in AMA's Human Resources Management Development Handbook (1994). Several other Crisp formats for his work on mentoring including a training video, a computer assisted training package, and his training program on computer disc.

Gordon and his associates in PRIME Systems Company also consult and train managers and executive teams on setting up mentoring programs and how to apply the skills and knowledge contained in his other books and training materials.

BOOKS BY GORDON SHEA PUBLISHED BY CRISP

Mentoring
Third Edition   A Fifty-Minute Book   ISBN 1-56052-642-4
A brief guide to the many styles of mentoring with the sage advice, worksheets, and information that can help refine the skills of a mentor.

Making the Most of Being Mentored
A Fifty-Minute Book   ISBN 1-56052-546-0
A companion book that guides the person being mentored to use to gain the maximum from this vital experience.

DATE DUE